HELLOFLO

the Guide,

PERIOD.

HELLOFLO

the Guide, PERIOD.

Written by
NAAMA BLOOM

Illustrated by
FLEUR SCIORTINO

DUTTON CHILDREN'S BOOKS

Dutton Children's Books

PENGUIN YOUNG READERS GROUP

An imprint of Penguin Random House LLC

375 Hudson Street

New York, NY 10014

Library of Congress Cataloging-in-Publication Data

Names: Bloom, Naama, author.

Title: Helloflo: the guide, period. / by Naama Bloom.

Description: New York, NY : Dutton Children's Books, [2017]

Identifiers: LCCN 2017025228| ISBN 9780399187292 (paperback)

ISBN 9780399187315 (hardcover) | ISBN 9780399187308 (ebook)

Subjects: LCSH: Puberty. | Teenage girls—Health and hygiene.

Teenage girls—Physiology.

BISAC: JUVENILE NONFICTION / Health & Daily Living / Maturing.

JUVENILE NONFICTION / Girls & Women.

JUVENILE NONFICTION / Health & Daily Living / Personal Hygiene.

Classification: LCC QP84.4 .B56 2017 | DDC 612.6/61—dc23

LC record available at https://lccn.loc.gov/2017025228

Printed in China

ISBN 9780399187292 (paperback)   10 9 8 7 6 5

ISBN 9780399187315 (hardcover)   10 9 8 7 6 5

Edited by Julie Strauss-Gabel

Design by Anna Booth

Text set in Feijoa

For the awkward girls trying to figure things out.

It gets better, I promise.

HELLOFLO

the Guide,

PERIOD.

Table of Contents

INTRODUCTION

There is no such thing as clean underwear. At least for a girl. You may start your day with a nice, fresh pair of underwear, but by your first trip to the bathroom? Yup, there's always something crusty waiting for you.

Sometimes less crusty than cottage-cheesy.

Sometimes less cottage-cheesy than yogurty.

It can often feel a bit like your body has taken it upon itself to produce its own personal dairy section. If you know what it's for, it can be magical (some might even say vagical). If you don't, it's shameful, confounding, embarrassing. But it's there. Always.

Being a girl is messy business. A fact widely known, though rarely discussed, by half the world's population. At nearly every stage of a girl's development something is spurting or sprouting or budding or blossoming. Garden metaphors abound! Based solely on evidence provided by decades of "feminine hygiene" advertisements, you'd be forgiven for concluding that getting your period is basically a monthly frolic through a field of sweet-smelling flowers.

But have you ever actually spent any time in a garden? It is dirty business. Literally. Plus, there are thorns and worms and, if you know anything about gardening, likely some sort of manure. So while it's not a perfect field of sweet-smelling flowers, a real garden may actually be the perfect metaphor. Puberty is messy business.

Oh, and there will be blood. A lot of it. Think: horror movie. Sometimes it may look and feel like a waterfall of blood when in actual fact you merely overslept and your maxi pad, the one that all the commercials tell you is so good at absorption, was simply not up to the task of your heavy flow day. Some people call those ruined panties "period underwear" and only pull them out of the drawer each month as needed. We like to think of them as our Red Badges of Courage.

And while we're on the topic of maxi pads, can we discuss the blue dye that we see in commercials as proof that the pads work? Since you probably haven't gotten your period yet, I want to let you in on a little secret: the blood you'll see when you get your period—it's not blue. In fact, sometimes it's not red. It can be all sorts of shades from red to brown. Just being honest here. You'll find that's the tone of this whole book.

So why does puberty get such a clean rap in all the commercials? Why do we usually talk about what happens to our bodies as though actual *information* is a tampon we need to quietly slip up our sleeves when we walk across the room? I'm not really sure. But what I do know is that it needs to change.

Girls, bear with me for a moment—we need to loop in your grown-ups.

ADULTS:

The girl sitting next to you is smart. She needs to know what's about to happen. Good thing you bought this book because I can guarantee the information she needs isn't at the bottom of a Yahoo Answers rabbit hole. It's a bit like reading *Are You There God? It's Me, Margaret* had it been written on the bathroom wall of Penn Station. With a Sharpie. Think that's an exaggeration? Please pause here for a moment and go Google pubic hair.

See?

Thanks to the prevalence of unrestricted pornography

on the Internet it's nearly impossible to Google anything about female anatomy without being immediately confronted by pornographic images. In fact, some studies suggest that children are encountering online porn as young as eight. *Not your children, of course, never your children.* But the children they know and talk to and play with. That's because online porn is the contemporary equivalent of your friend's older brother's contraband issue of *Playboy* that somehow made its way to your sixth-grade sleepover.

But even without those images there is simply *so much* information out there. How can a curious young girl, in search of answers about the changes she is experiencing, going to be able to differentiate between what is true and what she finds on the fourth page of a grammar-free message board?

I believe it's critical for your girl to understand what's happening to her own body. She needs to know that the world may start treating her differently just because she now looks like a woman. She also needs to know the basic essential fact that puberty is connected to reproduction. If she's not armed with this information she will have a much harder time processing the world around her and making good decisions. So take a deep breath and kindly hand the book back to her.

OKAY, GIRLS, BACK TO YOU.

As founder of HelloFlo.com I've been in the unique position to hear from thousands of girls and women about how they relate to their own bodies, and I've come to realize that the way we talk about physical changes is, well, lacking. I'm writing this book because you deserve honesty and real information. And you deserve to understand what's going on—both in your body and in the world around you.

That's why I've written this book. To supply you with all the facts, even the messy ones and the ones you may find most embarrassing to talk about. And I'm doing this in a way that acknowledges how intelligent and sophisticated you are.

Underlying everything HelloFlo does had been a determination to talk honestly with young women about what is happening with their bodies. No euphemisms, no avoidance, no blue dye.

We also celebrate it. Puberty is not a curse. It's confusing, uncomfortable, sometimes painful, but also interesting and ultimately powerful and empowering. It's like if a Girl Punk Band made a musical and your body was the orchestra. All Girl. All Punk. All power. That's what this book is—Punk Rock Puberty.

There will be questions you were afraid to ask and ones you didn't know even existed. There will be answers. There will be jokes. There will be stories. Many true, sometimes mortifying, stories. There will be pictures. There will be drawings. There will be Instagrams. There will be Beyoncé. And most definitely there will be blood.

As corny as this sounds, it's my dream that every girl enters puberty with enough knowledge of what's going on in her body and mind to keep her confident throughout. I've spoken to countless doctors, parents, and girls while writing this book, and I've tried to put everything that's useful in these pages. I'm not a doctor, I'm not even an expert. What I am is a woman who was once a confused girl who made it her mission to remove some of that confusion for the girls that came after me.

CHAPTER 1

GIRL, YOU'LL BE A
Woman
SOON

How soon is soon?

One year? Five years? Thirty minutes?

Let's start with the first question.

It's pretty much guaranteed that at some point your breasts will develop. Your period will arrive, and your body will start to bleed on a regular basis. (More on the bleeding later. I'll get to that.) It's also a sure thing to say you'll grow hair under your arms, between your legs, and on your legs. And these are just the changes you'll be able to see.

You may be thinking to yourself, that's a lot of changes. And you may be hoping that I can somehow tell you when to expect that change. I wish I could, but unfortunately I don't have that magical power. What I *can* tell you is what's behind all those changes and, hopefully, get you a bit more

WHAT'S GOING ON
in There?

BRAIN GROWTH SPURT

There's a lot happening in your brain during puberty! Discover what's going on upstairs in Chapter 7.

BREASTS

The next chapter is all about boobs! Check out pages 28–29 for the stages of breast development.

FIRST PERIOD

You'll start getting your period . . . sometime. Flip to Chapter 5 to learn what to expect, and check out Chapter 6 for some advice on what to do about it.

HAIR EVERYWHERE

You'll start growing pubic hair between your legs, and a different kind of body hair under your arms and on your legs. Check out Chapters 3 and 4 to learn more.

GROWTH SPURT

You'll get taller during puberty, and you might notice your feet and hands growing, too.

prepared to deal with them, perhaps even embrace them, when they come.

You are going to hear this a lot throughout this book, but the fact is that everyone's body is different and everyone has her own clock. This is an important thing to remember in life, not just about puberty. The truth is, so much of preparing for womanhood is preparing for things to happen to your body over which you have very little control. I can give you a rough idea of when these changes will start to occur, and in what order they will arrive, but that's about as good as a timetable gets.

Yes, it's frustrating. Yes, it would be nice if we were all born with a timetable we could look at in advance (Period Arrival time: Dec. 12, 1:15 p.m.), but that's not how things work.

The trick to dealing with puberty is to not give yourself a timetable. Try hard not to measure yourself by what's going on with your friends. Your friends' bodies are their own and have nothing to do with yours. Some may develop earlier than yours, some may develop later. Whatever your timetable, it will be right. Because it's right for you.

BUT WHAT'S
NORMAL?

*P*uberty can begin anywhere from eight to sixteen years old. That's a big span of time. Yes, the average age for first period is twelve years old, but remember how an average is calculated, it's all the numbers in the range added up and then divided by the actual number of data points. The average of twenty and eighty is fifty. See how that works? Fifty isn't particularly close to either of those numbers. This is important because many girls (and their parents) use that number twelve as some sort of goalpost for determining if they are normal. But you're normal even when you aren't the average.

If you're still caught up with the question of when, there is one factor that might be helpful. It's really the only one, and it's definitely not perfect. If you have access to them, ask your biological mother or aunts when they started experiencing the different parts of puberty. But even with that

The average age of first period in the Western world has been getting lower, from an average of seventeen over a century ago to around twelve today.

What Happens When?

AGE (YEARS)

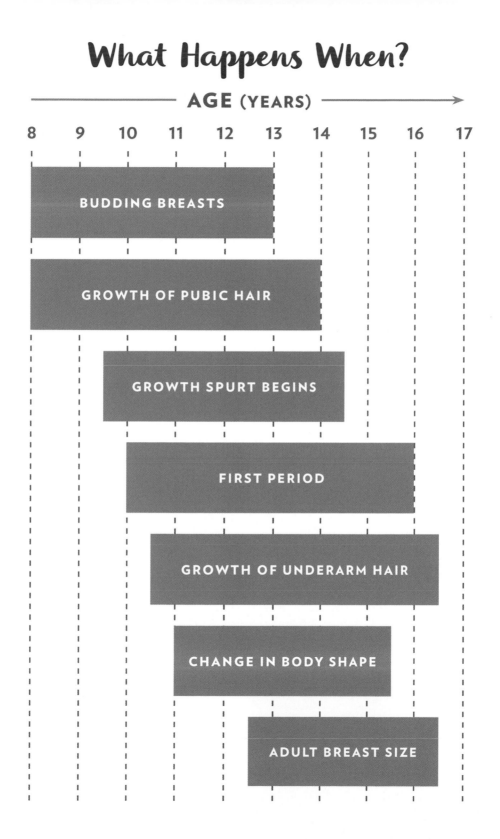

8   9   10   11   12   13   14   15   16   17

BUDDING BREASTS

GROWTH OF PUBIC HAIR

GROWTH SPURT BEGINS

FIRST PERIOD

GROWTH OF UNDERARM HAIR

CHANGE IN BODY SHAPE

ADULT BREAST SIZE

information, I'm sorry to say it's not a guarantee the same will happen to you. One of the factors for the lack of precision is that the way we are living now is very different from the way your mother and aunts grew up. Not that long ago, puberty would arrive similar to a line of falling dominoes. Your breasts would start developing, you'd get hair under your arms, your period would arrive— all in the course of a year or two.

The scientific term for first period is *menarche.*

Now, however, doctors are noticing that puberty begins much earlier than it used to and lasts much longer. So you may get breasts but then not get your period for another three years. Scientists aren't sure why this is happening. It may have something to do with all the light we're exposed to—think about it. One hundred years ago some people didn't even have electricity let alone an iPhone they took to bed—that's interfering with our sleep and growth patterns. It may also have something to do with the food we eat and how it's cultivated. It may even be from the chemicals in the air or water. It may be from all of these factors working together or something I haven't mentioned. There are many theories, but no one has the answer yet.

The point is, it's harder than ever to predict when

puberty will start and how long it will last. While there's never really been such a thing as *normal,* even the normal ranges we used to refer to no longer apply the way they did. Your body is running a solo show here. All you can do is pay attention, and be prepared.

Eau de Puberty

Here's one thing you can count on as far as puberty goes: You will probably know it's coming from the smell.

One of the first things that happens when hormones are released is that they cause you to sweat more. So you may find yourself sweating under your arms, or between your legs, or even on the bottoms of your feet and between your toes.

And while those hormones are only producing sweat, they are likely to soon be moving on to other things like producing hair under your arms, and breasts under your nipples. Though, like I said earlier, it's not clear when they will decide to get around to this. Just know that they are on their way.

Also a little PSA (Public Service Announcement), I'm not trying to make you paranoid but every fifth-grade teacher I've ever spoken to has told me one thing. Their classrooms stink! That's because all the kids are starting to sweat but not everyone is using soap in the shower. So do your teacher a favor, USE SOAP!

RUBE GOLDBERG
MACHINE

A Rube Goldberg machine is a great metaphor for hormones—it's a complicated piece of machinery that is designed to perform a relatively simple task. The machine works through a series of chain reactions. Chain reactions are what we need to talk about now. I'm going to oversimplify here, so bear with me. In your body, the machine that triggers the chain reaction known as puberty is your ovaries. Actually, it really starts with an area of your brain called the hypothalamus. The hypothalamus releases a hormone that causes the pituitary gland to release a hormone that, essentially, wakes up the ovaries. We'll talk about the other function of ovaries later but for now here's what you need to know.

Until you enter puberty your ovaries are basically like lightbulbs that have been dimmed really, really low: They're there, but they're not doing a whole lot of anything. Then, when you begin puberty, the volume is turned up a little bit and they start to go to work. And by start to work, I mean they produce those hormones. When the ovaries start making estrogen and progesterone, the hormones then travel all over the body and tell different parts of the body to do different things—breast development, hair growth, hip widening, and periods. It's one very complicated chain reaction.

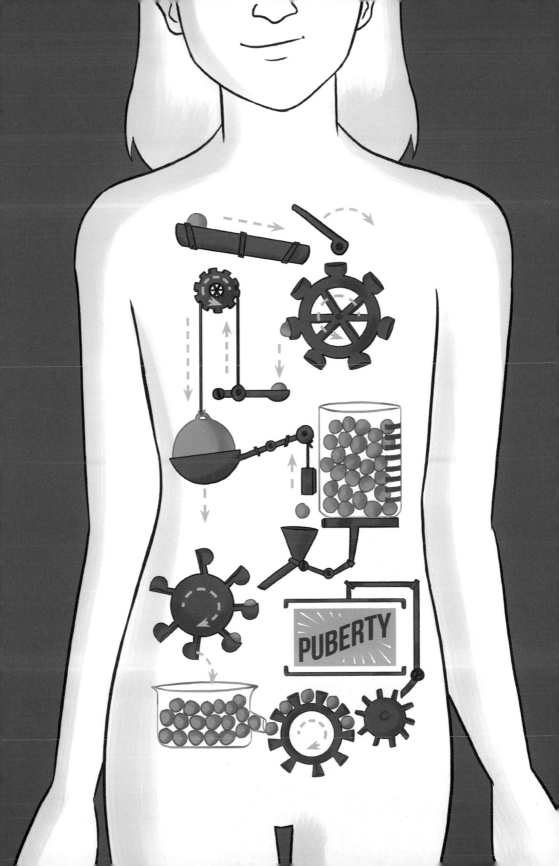

W-O-M-A-N-?

Most of what we've discussed so far is mechanical. Hormones are released, and a series of chain reactions cause your body to change. It's all pretty simple when you look at it that way. But another way to look at it is that the chain reaction also starts you on the path to adulthood—or rather, womanhood.

So what does woman really mean? In my opinion this is actually one of the most important psychological aspects

of puberty. Everyone starts saying you're a woman. But really, you're still a kid and you should enjoy being a kid.

What's different is that your body is preparing itself for doing grown-up things—like being able to have a baby.

But that doesn't mean you're *ready* to have a baby. You may not be ready to have a baby for a long, long, long time. You may never want to have a baby.

Just remember that the ability to have a baby does not mean you're no longer a kid. It just means that you're a kid whose ovaries have started producing hormones.

BUT
HOW WILL IT FEEL?
CAN YOU TELL ME?

Yes, I can tell you how it's going to feel. Or at least I can give you a good idea of how it will feel. And I will. In each chapter we'll talk about how the changes might affect your day-to-day life, and how to deal with each of these changes so that you feel like you're in control of your own body. The more you know what's going on, and what will go on, the less scary everything will be (this is true in life also). And a lot of these things might not be scary at all! Sure, sometimes some of these changes might feel uncomfortable, but they won't ever keep you from doing the things you want to do. It's just a matter of being prepared.

And that's what this book is about. It's about explaining to you exactly what is going on in your body, and all the different ways you can take care of it. And like I said earlier, I'm going to tell it to you honestly and won't use any euphemisms because nothing about this topic embarrasses me, and it shouldn't embarrass you, either.

Dr. Laura C. Torchen,
ENDOCRINOLOGIST

1. **What hormones have to be present for puberty to begin?**
   There are two major classes of sex hormones. These are the estrogen and the androgen. Testosterone is in the androgen family of hormones. Body odor and sexual hair, like pubic hair and axillary hair, are all androgen-mediated changes. Usually about two years before the onset of puberty, the adrenal glands start to produce more of those androgen types of hormones. In a subset of kids, when this happens, they'll actually have some symptoms—they could develop acne or body odor or even axillary or pubic hair. We call that *adrenarche*. It's not directly linked to puberty, although kids who have earlier adrenarche tend to have earlier puberty and usually once adrenarche starts we know that puberty will follow.

ESTROGEN

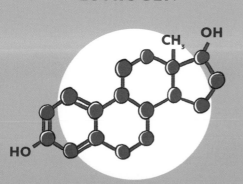

TESTOSTERONE

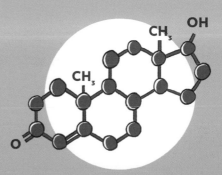

2. What is "early puberty"?

Right now the definition of early puberty that the Pediatric
Endocrine Society uses for a girl is younger than age eight. That
means girls experiencing puberty at eight is the youngest range
of normal.

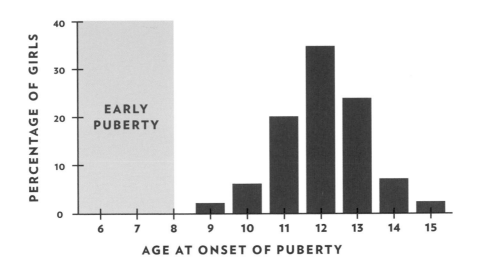

In my friend group I was one of the last to get my period, so all my friends would have these conversations, like, "I started today" or "My cramps are really bad." I felt so left out. Part of me wanted to get my period so that I could fit in and the other part of me wanted it so I would feel like a grown-up. I would even have myself convinced that my boobs hurt or because I had to pee so much, I was definitely about to start.

Eve

I'm happy and kind of sad that my body is changing. Sometimes it hurts—like, your boobs hurt or you get cramps. But I also like it because it's the right time and I'm growing up. Last summer when I was ten, I realized that all my friends were changing, too. We talked about it a lot. My really close friend is further ahead in the process than us, so it's nice to hear her talk about it.

Claude

You know in your chest how there's the sternum? I used to always see that little bump when I looked in the mirror—it didn't really mean much to me but it was a part of my body. Then when I started getting boobs, I couldn't see it as much—it wasn't prominent anymore. I started feeling emotional about it. It was a small thing, but my body was changing, and I felt like I didn't get to control it.

Isabel

CHAPTER 2

Bustin' Out

(OR NOT)

Boobs. We're talking about these first for three reasons. First, they are one of the earliest signs that puberty has begun. Second, they are one of the most obvious signs. Lastly, they have cultural significance—not *your* breasts exactly—but all breasts. Meaning, the world seems obsessed with them, and I want you to understand why. Though admittedly I can only theorize on that last point.

Your developing breasts are the most visible sign to the outside world that you're going through puberty. This stinks because there is so much happening that you probably want to process in private, and it may feel like your body is betraying you. We've all been there. And I'm not going to sugarcoat—it can feel awkward.

Sometimes it can seem like you're the only one

ALL PRIMATES HAVE
Breasts

This means men and apes as well as women! The difference is when women go through puberty a rise in estrogen causes female breasts to enlarge, whereas testosterone keeps men's flat. In nonhuman female primates the breasts only become swollen when they are suckling their babies.

stumbling through this and everyone else has it under control. But if there's one thing I've learned since starting Hello-Flo and hearing from so many girls, it's this: *Everyone* feels like they are stumbling awkwardly through puberty. Even the cool girls, the pretty girls, and the popular girls. In fact, even the boys are struggling to deal with their own changing bodies.

Okay, back to the subject at hand, boobs. What's the big deal about boobs?

Sometimes it can feel like everything, and I mean *everything*, comes down to breasts. How big they are, what shape they are, whether they look like the ones on television. And also, when are they coming, already? Or, how come they came so soon!? Not to mention, why is everyone so obsessed with them?

In 783 CE, Saxon women, including noble-born Fastrada, famously hurled themselves bare-breasted into battle against Charlemagne's forces. Fastrada later became Charlemagne's third wife and queen of the Franks.

The reality is that there is no getting away from your breasts. Some girls get them very young. Some girls feel like they have to wait *forever* for them to arrive. Some women have large ones and spend their lives feeling uncomfortable and wishing they were smaller, some women remain flat chested and dream of the busty life. No matter how you may feel about them, your breasts are a part of you. But you are not your breasts. They're just two somewhat-round puzzle pieces that make up the whole picture of you.

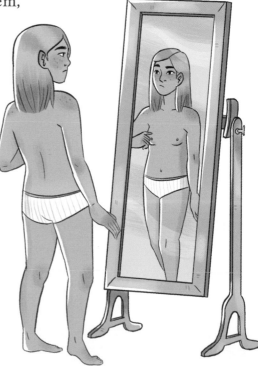

WHY DO WE HAVE
BREASTS?

The primary biological function of breasts is to nurse children. Like most changes that occur during puberty, the end goal is to facilitate and support the creation of new life. Mother Nature is very keen on keeping the planet full of humans. But breastfeeding is likely not something you will have to worry about for a long time, if ever. So let's talk about what your breasts are doing now.

There are five stages of breast development and they happen at a different pace for everyone. Some girls zoom through each stage and appear to develop breasts practically overnight, others can take nearly a decade.

Because it can be so easy to see where everyone else falls on this timeline, the state of your own breasts might cause you some anxiety. But before you run to the bathroom to stuff toilet paper in your training bra (believe me, I can tell you from experience, it's *never* a good look) or strap them down with some industrial tape (just, OUCH), please remember that, as with everything concerning your body, the only right way is *your* way.

Here's what's happening: When you begin to go through puberty your body experiences a rise in a hormone called estrogen (we alluded to this earlier). The increased estrogen causes the growth of mammary glands, which are located behind your nipples and are the glands that will later be responsible for producing milk. These glands are connected to your nipple through a series of milk ducts. After childbirth, these glands will supply the milk to the nipple. Fat develops around these glands to protect them. It's this fat that makes up most of what we consider our breasts.

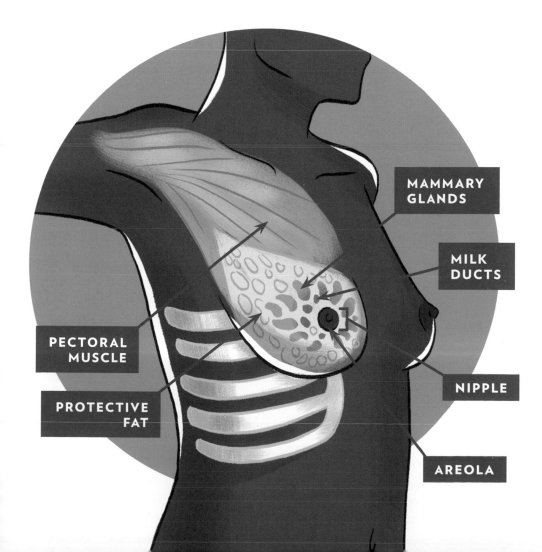

WHEN?
(WHEN WHEN WHEN WHEN????)

There are five typical stages to breast development. Not everyone will experience all five stages; some girls skip steps.

STAGE ONE
Nothing to see here

Prepuberty you have no breasts and have not yet begun to produce estrogen or develop mammary glands. The very, very early signs of puberty may be beginning inside the body, but there are no outward signs.

STAGE TWO
Hey, buddy

Between ages eight and eleven, estrogen will begin to circulate in your body, and your mammary glands will form. Your nipples and areola will get larger and begin to protrude forming small buds that may feel like lumps under your nipples. It's not unusual for one "bud" to form before the other, so don't panic if you look down and see one nipple popping farther out than the other.

STAGE THREE
C'mon, get fatty

During this phase fat deposits will begin to form around your mammary glands. Your breasts may begin to appear pointy, and you may decide it's time to start wearing a bra. Where these fat deposits develop, how big, and what shape they are varies from person to person and will determine the size and shape of your breasts.

STAGE FOUR
Attention!

Some women never experience stage four at all and skip right over it. Others may stop right here. If you are a stage four-er your nipple and areola will continue to grow and form a separate mound, causing your breasts to appear pointy or cone shaped.

STAGE FIVE
Final destination

Behold your breasts. While breasts may change somewhat in shape and size due to weight gain or loss, pregnancy, and nursing, by stage five you basically have the breasts you will have for life. Be nice to them. Treat them with kindness and love. You're in it together for the long haul.

STACKING UP

It's almost inevitable that you will compare your breasts to the girls and women around you, whether they are your friends, the people you see on TV, on Instagram, in magazines, or on Facebook. It's natural for people to look to others to see where they fit in the world—we all do it, so give yourself a break. However, sometimes it's easy to get confused and think the measure of your breasts is the same as the measure of you as a person.

Here's a quick reminder: **THEY ARE NOT**.

You will hear me say this over and over, but one of the reasons I'm writing this book is because I want to save you some of the worry and anguish I experienced when I was going through puberty. I want to pass on some of the secrets it took me years to learn. Ready?

Here's another big one: How *you* feel about your body will determine how everyone else feels about it. I know it's hard to believe—but it's true! And it happens to be one

of the great truths that smart, confident, beautiful women learn as they get older, and wish they had known when they were younger. I *wish* I had known this when I was growing up. It would have saved me SO much time and worry (not to mention bad, trendy jean purchases). Still skeptical? How about this: Think of the most beautiful woman you know. Now think what makes her beautiful. You may think that it has something to do with her hair, her body, her breast size. But, really, when you think about it, it almost always

Nipples

Nipples may be the smallest part of your breast, but they can be a big deal. I get a lot of questions from girls about whether their nipples are normal (see Dr. Ross's Q&A on page 37). The thing is, much like your breasts, nipples can come in all shapes and sizes. Some are big, some dark, some small. Some can also be very sensitive, others not so much. Also, it's totally normal to have some hair around your nipples. Lots of girls and women do.

OVER-THE-SHOULDER
Boulder Holder
OR, WHEN IS IT TIME TO
Get a Bra?

When to buy your first bra is a personal decision and one you should likely discuss with your grown-up. Megan Grassell, who started the bra company Yellowberry, suggests the best time is when you start budding and you find that running around or playing sports can be a little bit uncomfortable. If you're someone who's developed early and you are uncomfortable wearing a bra, or worry you will stand out, there are plenty of options like sports bras or tank bras that provide the same amount of support but don't *look* like a bra.

has to do with her confidence in herself.

How do you get that much confidence in yourself? I promised honesty, so I'll be truthful and tell you I'm still figuring it out. But what my personal experience has taught me is that I feel most confident when I force myself to stop worrying about what other people want me to be or look like and start focusing on what I want to do.

Also it's useful to know that for even the most confident person, the barrage of what you see in magazines and on the Internet can make you feel like there is only one way to look and other ways are wrong or not as good. And since everywhere you look there seems to be breasts, it's understandable you might think yours should look a certain way.

When those moments strike, the first thing I'd like you to keep in mind is that the best breast is a healthy breast. Quick put this book down and say it ten times: *The best breast is a healthy breast!*

Done? Okay. The next thing I want you to remember is that in the *real* world, breasts come in all shapes and sizes. No two are alike. Sometimes not even the ones on your own body. In fact, it's not unusual for your breasts to be slightly different in size and shape, sometimes noticeably so. On very rare occasions they can even be different cup sizes. Oftentimes, breasts can swell and become sensitive leading up to your period, and once your period is over they return to their normal size. You may feel these changes are overwhelming and obvious when they happen, but almost always they will only be noticeable to you.

The word *brassiere* was first coined in 1907 in *Vogue* magazine

Also it's important to remember that at different points in history people had different views on what the *perfect* breast size should be. In Ancient Egypt small breasts were

the rage, in Ancient Greece the fashion was definitely busty. In the 1960s in America there was Twiggy, and in the 1990s there was Kate Moss; both were the biggest supermodels in the world and both were flat-chested. In the 1950s there was Marilyn Monroe and now we have Kim Kardashian, both of whom are, er, busting out. Here's another thing. Hold

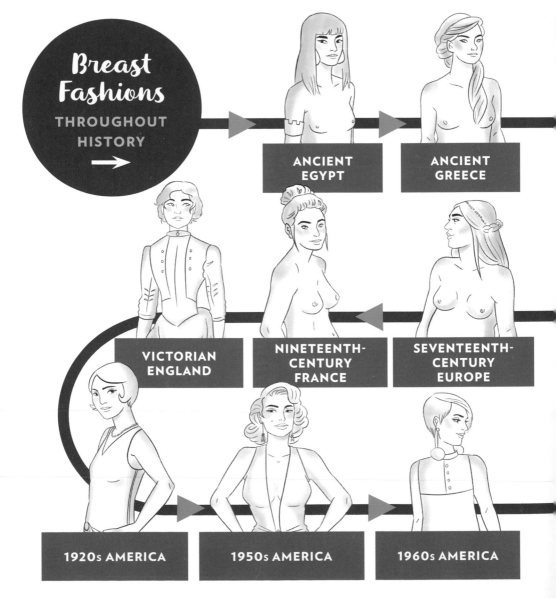

Breast Fashions THROUGHOUT HISTORY →

ANCIENT EGYPT

ANCIENT GREECE

VICTORIAN ENGLAND

NINETEENTH-CENTURY FRANCE

SEVENTEENTH-CENTURY EUROPE

1920s AMERICA

1950s AMERICA

1960s AMERICA

up, are you thinking those women lucked out because they just happened to be born with the type of breast that people thought were fashionable at the time? Not true! When each of these women became well known, their shape was the exact opposite of what was in fashion at the time; they just owned what they had. And the rest is history. Or herstory.

ASK**FLO**

> I got my period but I'm still flat chested—
> when will I get boobs?

The short answer is you have breasts already. But if you're asking when will they get larger, the answer is maybe never. But don't be discouraged. Some women get super large breasts, others get tiny breasts, and some are right in the middle. All are beautiful if the person "wearing them" is confident. Trust me—your friend over there with the really large breasts—wishes hers were more like yours.

> How do I ask my mom to start
> letting me wear a push-up bra?

This is a tricky one, and unfortunately for you, one that we're going to turn around on you. Before asking your grown-up to take you shopping for a push-up or padded bra, you might want to ask yourself why you want to wear one in the first place.

Tough question, we know. The thing is, what you have is great and while everyone likes to enhance what they have every now and then, it's important to understand our motivations for doing so. When you have an answer that feels good to you, talk about it with your grown-up and see if they're on board.

Dr. Sheryl Ross,
GYNECOLOGIST

1. **Are there any tips for taking care of your breasts long term?**

   We have all heard the saying, "you are what you eat." This can be applied to many medical conditions, including breast health. Eating a colorful diet, including a variety of fruits and vegetables, limiting alcohol and caffeine intake, not smoking, and controlling your weight have all been shown to improve breast health and lower your risk of getting breast cancer. Using a daily moisturizer on the skin of your breasts also contributes to healthy appearing breasts.

2. **Is there such a thing as a normal nipple?**

   During different stages of life and hormonal surges, nipples change in size and appearance. The majority of nipples point away from the body, while others, known as "inverted" nipples, point into the body. The belly button has a similar, "innie" vs. "outtie" variation. Nipple variations are more common. The same factors that affect breast size and shape also affect the appearance of the nipple. There is no such thing as "normal" nipples.

3. **Are there things I can do to make my breasts look different (not including surgery)?**

Lifestyle choices, including diet and healthy living, will help keep your body mass index (BMI) under 25 which helps keep your breast size consistent and true to their natural size. Medications such as the birth control pill and hormone replacement therapy can affect your breast tissue, making them slightly larger. Caffeine and nicotine stimulate fibrocystic densities in breast tissue increasing their size as well.

4. **Is it true that if you don't wear a bra you'll get saggy boobs?**

Poor support can lead to "saggy" breasts regardless of your size. If you don't wear an everyday bra, the delicate and sensitive breast tissue is unsupported, which may cause breasts to sag. If you choose to wear a bra, it should be properly fitted. Larger-breasted women (greater than a C cup) are more vulnerable to sagging if their breast tissue is unsupported over long periods of time. During exercise, a sports bra, with its stronger fabric and purposeful construction, provides additional care and comfort to breast tissue in motion. It should be noted, however, that some sagging is totally normal and can't be avoided as you age.

5. **Do young women need to give themselves breast exams?**

Yes, I believe it's important to know your breasts well, starting at an early age. During your first visit with the gynecologist, which should be around sixteen to eighteen years old, you should be shown how to do a breast self-exam. Breast tissue can be intimidating in the beginning, but once you are familiar with your own breast tissue and all its normal lumps and bumps, you will be able to find abnormal changes if they occur. The best time to check your breasts is during the first week of your period when the hormonal effects on breast tissue have subsided.

HOW TO

GIVE YOURSELF A
Breast Examination

You and your breasts are going to have a long relationship together so it's important to identify any changes in breast shape, size, skin changes, or nipple discharge. There are five steps of a breast self-exam. With each step you need to look at your breasts closely to identify any new changes.

STEP 1: Stand in front of the mirror with your hands on your hips.

STEP 2: Raise your arms over your head while looking for changes in the mirror.

STEP 3: Look for any discharge or fluid coming from the nipples.

STEP 4: Now lie on your back and feel each breast looking for lumps and unfamiliar tissue changes. Extend the hand over your head of the breast you are examining. Use the opposite hand, running your fingertips firmly over the breast tissue in a circular motion, about the size of a quarter. Think of the breast as a plus (+) sign, feeling each quarter in a purposeful way each month. Once you have finished examining each breast, check each underarm to feel for similar changes.

STEP 5: Now stand up or sit and recheck your breasts in a similar fashion as in Step 4.

Sometimes checking the breasts in the shower, when the skin is wet and slippery, helps identify abnormalities more easily.

As a young adult, I was self-conscious of my body. All of my friends had bigger breasts and I thought that meant there was something wrong with me. As I got older, I worked to appreciate *my* body more. And when I thought about all the times I wished I looked differently, wished I was a different girl, it seemed like such a waste of time.

Allyson

When I was nine years old, my breasts showed up abruptly and without my permission. I never got to be the girl who prayed for big boobs because I was the girl whose third-grade teacher had to call home and suggest I start wearing a bra. It seemed that overnight so many things became off-limits to me: running, flipping over, cartwheels. Basically anything that jostled these chest aliens felt like it became something only boys could do.

Ashley

This one time I came home, it must have been late May or early June and it must have been really hot out. It was so, so hot that I took off my shirt and marched around the house. My brother came home and said, "You know you can't do that anymore, right? You're going to get boobs." I knew he was right that I'd get them, but I was so mad that I didn't have any control, and that I had this predestined future.

Maggie

CHAPTER 3

BEATING AROUND THE
Bush

OR THE HAIR DOWN THERE

It happens to everyone. One day you're at the swimming pool, or changing for school, or getting out of the shower, and you glance down there and see hair that wasn't there before. Dark hair. Coarse hair. At first it's just a strand or two, but eventually, one hair turns into five and over time you develop a thick, triangular patch of curly hair between your legs where there was none before. Pubic hair has arrived.

This new hair might be really exciting to you, especially if you're a "late bloomer" (or even if you aren't). I remember being kind of excited when I spotted my first pubic hair because I thought it made me more of a grown-up. And I have a close friend whose son got his first pubic hair and was really excited to tell her about it. See, boys are focused on their puberty, too, it's not just you.

LET'S START WITH SOME
BASIC FACTS

*P*ubic hair is a part of puberty. Like all other parts of puberty, everyone develops pubic hair at a different rate. Generally speaking, you will begin to notice strands of coarse hair appearing in your pubic area around the same time you notice your breasts beginning to develop, but likely before you get your period. Chances are this hair will also start to appear before you get any hair under your arms, and it won't start to get curlier and thicker until you are nearly done with puberty. Also, your pubic hair may not be the same color as the hair on your head and may actually be much darker.

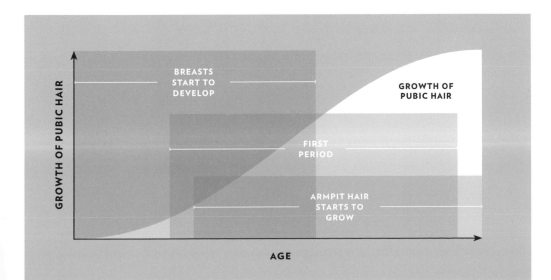

BUT WHY IS IT
THERE?

*N*ow that you know what it is and when to expect it, you might still be wondering why we have pubic hair. The answer, unfortunately, is not very clear.

There are a lot of theories about why humans have pubic hair, but the truth is no one knows for sure. One theory is that the first appearance of pubic hair dates back to the time of Neanderthals, and we grew it in order to keep our reproductive organs warm. This theory seems less likely because it would also imply that women would need to have hairy bellies to cover their ovaries and uterus and men would have hairy penises, which we know is not the case. Others have speculated that pubic hair serves the same function as nose hair, namely to keep the dirt out of our private parts. This theory may make sense for women— pubic hair protects a girl's vulva and urethra—but doesn't work as well for men; their urethra is at the end of their penis and hairless.

The most likely theory is that pubic hair plays a role in attracting the opposite sex for the purpose of reproduction. So, believe it or not, it may actually exist in order to help us further the human species.

Now, Hang in There

Humans have two types of sweat glands: *eccrine glands*, which are all over our body and are the glands that produce the sweat that keeps us cool when we exercise or are in hot places, and the *apocrine glands*. The apocrine glands can only be found under our arms and, you guessed it, in the same places where we grow pubic hair. These glands only appear during puberty. When the secretions produced by the apocrine glands mix with bacteria caught in underarm or pubic hair the result is body odor.

ECCRINE GLANDS are all over the body and used for cooling.

APOCRINE GLANDS are only under the arms and near the groin.

Think of body odor as your own personal scent. Technically speaking, your odor—picture a perfume bottle with your face on it—is partially determined by a set of genes called the major histocompatibility complex, or MHC. What's interesting is that each person has their own particular aroma, and there is research to suggest it is this scent that attracts other people (whether they know it or not). Several studies have shown that when women are asked to sniff men's shirts that have been worn for a few days the smell they find most appealing belongs to men with a totally different scent (or MHC) from their own. This is good for reproduction. Years and years ago when people's worlds were much smaller, it wasn't so unlikely that relatives would get married and have children. This scent was mother nature's way of steering us away from people with a similar genetic makeup.

WHO PUT THE *L* IN PUBIC?

Years ago, before Instagram, my friend's eight-year-old son once asked her, "Mom, if it's on your private parts, why is it called pub-lic hair?" At the time she told me this, we just laughed about how cute his comment was, but now I think he was onto something.

Over the past few years, because of our nonstop ac-cess to nude (or practically

The first pubic hair to appear in a painting was Goya's *The Nude Maja* in 1800. He was later put on trial by the Spanish Inquisition because of it.

nude) images of just about everyone on the Internet, it seems that what to do with your pubic hair has become a public conversation. I wish this wasn't the case, but it is. And because of this reality, I'm going to address it head on. I wrote this book because I believe with all my heart that you need to have information so that you can put what's going on with your body into the proper context. This will help you make the decisions for your body that feel right for YOU.

If after reading this chapter you still have questions or don't know what you want for yourself, it's *always* okay to ask. Just promise me that when it comes to pubic hair, and your body in general, you only ask these questions of

Pubic Hair Fashions

THROUGHOUT HISTORY

→

ANCIENT EGYPT

ANCIENT GREECE

people you really know and trust. These are not questions to be crowd-sourced online.

First of all, you should know that you are not the first person to wonder about this. The conversation about pubic hair has been going on for nearly as long as people have been growing it. So, basically, always.

Want proof? Just head over to your local museum or art book section in the library. The first thing to remember—and this is true with so much that has to do with our physical appearance, private and otherwise—is that what is in fashion or considered "normal" is usually connected to humans wanting to project an image of health, wealth, and power. For instance, have you ever wondered why women

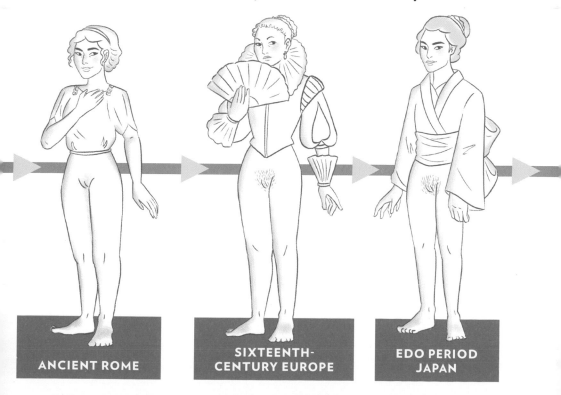

ANCIENT ROME

SIXTEENTH-
CENTURY EUROPE

EDO PERIOD
JAPAN

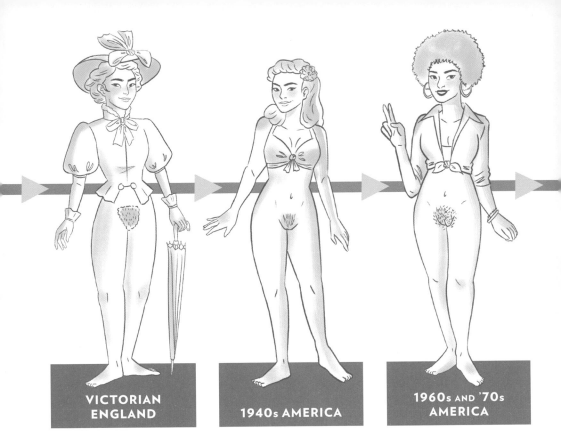

in the paintings you see in museums often look plump? (Or "Rubenesque," as the artists like to say.)

This is because for many centuries a full figure was considered a sign of wealth; only the poor and starving were skinny. The same idea applies to pubic hair "fashion." The Egyptians removed body hair using a form of depilatory cream and waxing because they felt it reflected cleanliness, youth, and health. The Greeks and Romans did the same thing.

But by the fifteenth century, the more pubic hair a person had, the better. At the time syphilis, a sexually transmitted disease that led to blindness, insanity, or even death,

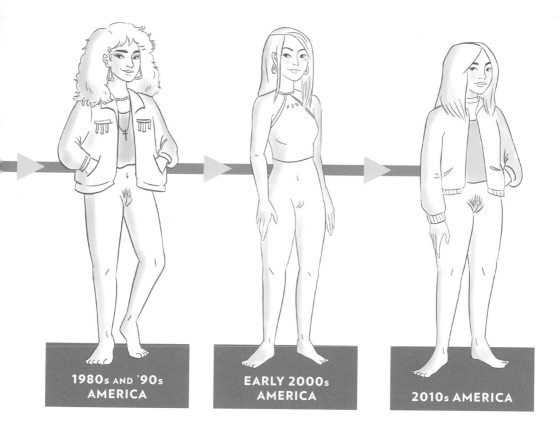

1980s AND '90s
AMERICA

EARLY 2000s
AMERICA

2010s AMERICA

was rampant. The only known treatment for it was mercury, which caused people to lose their pubic hair. At the same time, women would often trim or shave their pubic hair to either combat pubic lice or make themselves less susceptible to it. For both of these reasons, a full growth of pubic hair was a symbol of a clean bill of health.

Humans have as many hair follicles as apes.

To cover up (literally!) these health issues something called the *merkin*, basically a pubic hair wig, was invented.

In the first half of the twentieth century, with the advent

of razors and bikinis, removing some pubic hair once again became fashionable. In the 1970s, at the height of the women's liberation movement, a full growth of pubic hair came back into fashion and was often considered a sign of a strong independent woman. In recent years, bikini waxes have become very popular. So you see, whatever you decide to do with your pubic hair, it has likely been done before.

Things today are a bit confusing. There are some women who have chosen to be completely bare, others who shave just the hairs that stick out when they are wearing a bathing suit, and still others who go "full bush." All of these choices are personal and all are completely normal. As with everything else about your body, you need to do what feels right for you. Not what you think other people want you to do.

The technical term for the appearance of pubic hair is *pubarche*.

But the real reason for the confusion today is that women's choices about their pubic hair are on display more than ever. I don't mean that people are walking around naked, but I do mean that pictures of naked women are often just a Google search away. And this fact has created an environment where everyone seems to have an opinion about what a woman should do with her pubic hair.

The most important answer to the question of how to care for your pubic hair is this: whatever you are comfortable with. However, if you are asking the question you may not know yet what makes you comfortable, and that's okay, too. The truth is you may be comfortable with different things at different times in your life. There's only one answer that is always right: You shouldn't do anything that makes you *uncomfortable*. You're going to hear this answer a lot when it comes to decisions about your body and adulthood, but that doesn't make it less true. Part of becoming an adult is learning what you like and don't like and being okay with it.

I have many friends who used to remove their pubic hair but have stopped because they want their daughters to see that pubic hair is normal. Some women shave off some and trim the rest. Some prefer to remove it all. And I have one friend who years ago chose to laser her hair off and now wishes she hadn't done so.

People do all of these things at different times in their lives.

BUT IS IT SAFE
TO REMOVE PUBIC HAIR?

Yes. If done correctly and cleanly, removing pubic hair is generally safe. Sometimes removing pubic hair can result in rashes or ingrown hair which appear as red bumps, and it may take a while to figure out what works best for you. When you first decide to try removing your pubic hair, it's a good idea to talk to a grown-up.

If you do decide to remove any of your pubic hair, you have options to consider.

TOOLS OF THE
TRADE

- **SHAVING:** Using a razor to shave it off is the least expensive, and usually least painful, way to remove pubic hair. But it also requires you do it frequently, usually every week.

- **WAXING:** This is usually done by a professional, and involves spreading wax thinly over sections of your pubic hair, applying cloth or paper on top of it, and then ripping it off. It is more painful than other options (you probably already guessed that) and more expensive, but the hair takes longer to grow back, usually four to six weeks.

BIKINI WAX: When the pubic hair outside where your underwear or bathing suit covers up is waxed off.

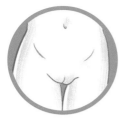

BRAZILIAN WAX: Removes all or mostly all of your pubic hair. Sometimes a thin strip of hair is left down the middle of your vulva.

- **SUGARING:** Sugaring has been practiced for centuries and is similar to waxing, but instead of wax a mixture of sugar, lemon, and water is used to create a gel that is applied to the hair and then ripped off.

- **LASER HAIR REMOVAL:** Laser hair removal is permanent and very expensive and always done by a professional. A pulsating laser light is directed at the hair follicles, destroying them permanently.

- **DEPILATORY CREAMS:** These can be purchased at the drugstore and contain chemicals that remove the hair by dissolving it. They are a bit messy and can sometimes be harsh on sensitive skin.

I was a competitive swimmer from the time I was ten till I was sixteen. When I started growing hair down there—around age thirteen—I suddenly noticed that the older girls shaved their bikini lines. So, I bought some shaving cream and a razor and shaved it off enough so it wouldn't show. I don't recall ever having a conversation with my mother about it, it was just something I learned from watching all the other girls.

Glynnis

I remember I was going to the bathroom when I noticed that my vagina—actually my vulva—had hair on it. And that it felt really weird. Over the next few months, it gradually grew in and got fuller and fuller. Then I had fifth-grade health, and someone finally explained that this is pubic hair, and I remember thinking "Been there done that!"

Kate

I can vividly remember taking a shower with my mom when I was probably six or seven and wondering what was up with all that hair! So, I asked her why she had it, and she told me that it was something that women get, and that I'd start growing hair when I was in middle school. That was the only conversation I ever had with my mom about pubic hair, but she was right. I started noticing my own pubic hair when I was about twelve.

It went from a couple of strands to a full bush, so to speak, overnight. I didn't really know what to do with it, or if I had to do anything at all.

Kara

CHAPTER 4

AND EVEN MORE
Hair

Yup we're still talking about hair. Why am I spending so much time on this topic?

I have three reasons. First, your body is changing and the changes to your hair are one of the most obvious ways it's changing. Second, the world has opinions about your hair. I wish that wasn't true but it is. So in order for you to know how YOU want to manage your hair, you need to learn all about it. Third, just like pubic hair, I want you to see that all of these choices are influenced by trends and cultural norms, and they are always changing. For example, in the past ten years of my life, eyebrows have gone from thin and highly arched to thick and more straight, with a few stops along the way. These things are part of fashion, and you don't always have to conform to fashion to be fashionable.

FACIAL HAIR: Yep, women get it, too. One in four girls will get some kind of facial hair.

ARMPIT HAIR usually starts to appear after pubic hair and will grow thicker and darker throughout puberty.

PUBIC HAIR: Your crash course in body hair.

Like underarm hair, **LEG HAIR** starts to get thicker and darker during puberty.

SO,
TELL ME ABOUT IT

From reading the last chapter you already know about pubic hair. Think of pubic hair as your crash course in body hair. Sometime after you notice your pubic hair appearing, you will likely begin to see some darker hair under your arms. At first this hair may be light and soft, but after a while, a dark strand or two may appear. As you continue to go through puberty, this hair will increase in thickness.

The same will start to happen on your legs, particularly from the knee down. Most women (and men) are born with hair on their legs. It's often soft and fine and light in color. But similar to pubic and underarm hair, as you begin to develop this hair will grow darker and thicker. Not as thick as a man's, but thicker than it is now.

The Elizabethans also removed unwanted hair: the hair on their foreheads. In sixteenth-century England people believed a larger forehead signified intelligence and plucked away their head hair and eyebrows to give themselves the appearance of a larger brow.

FINE FINE.
BUT WHY?

Like many other things we've discussed, the answer is no one is quite sure. There are many theories to explain why we grow hair under our arms, but they are just that, theories.

One popular one is that hair prevents friction. When we walk or run our arms naturally rub against the skin on the sides of our bodies and some experts have theorized that hair keeps the skin from getting irritated.

Perhaps body hair is there to wick away moisture (i.e. sweat) from under our arms, at the same time pushing out the bacteria that creates body odor.

Or, like pubic hair, the hair under our arms may be there to carry the pheromones that invisibly attract us to others.

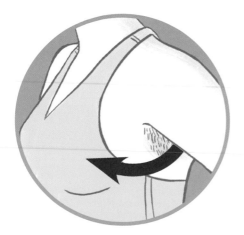

Is body hair there to reduce friction?

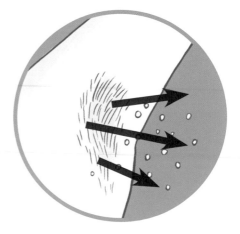

To wick away sweat?

A **pheromone** is an invisible chemical that we secrete, which causes a specific reaction in other humans. Some people think they are the secret ingredient to attraction.

The truth is we may never know for sure why this hair grows. The more important question is, why do we care so much about it?

Everyone, men and women, has a complicated relationship with their body hair, basically since it started to grow.

This is not entirely surprising. Hair is, after all, the most easily altered part of our body, and it has always been used to send messages—about beauty, about power, about politics.

But leg and underarm hair is actually a relatively recent addition to the roster of "unwanted hair," and in western countries our practice of getting rid of it is barely a century old.

Or is it there to help spread pheremones?

S hort, because American women didn't really start shaving under their arms until the early twentieth century. That may sound like a long time, but when you consider that we've been growing underarm and leg hair for a few millennia, a century is more like a hairbreadth in time.

Now that we've talked about how many beauty standards are shaped by trends, it shouldn't surprise you that we owe our determination to shave it away to fashion magazines. In 1915, just as women's fashions were beginning to loosen up and bare upper arms—which had previously been considered shocking—began to make an appearance in public, *Harper's Bazaar* published a photo of a model in a sleeveless dress dancing with her arms raised. The photo was part of an advertisement for hair-removal products. The suggestion was that to participate in something as fun and youthful as modern dancing, one needed hairless underarms. Depilatory cream and disposable razors were becoming widely available at the time and were more easily accessible. American women have been shaving under there more or less ever since.

Still, shaved underarms remained a very American trend until the mid-twentieth century. Italian screen goddess Sophia Loren was pictured in many glamour shots in the 1950s with thick underarm hair.

Leg hair hung on a bit longer. Even though skirts came up in the Twenties, flappers, the "it" girls of their day, did not feel that hairy legs interfered with their ability to have fun or look beautiful. It wasn't until the 1940s, when a combination of silk stockings and the popularity of Hollywood pinup stars posing with exposed legs inspired women to extend their shaving routines down the leg line.

The shaving trend was not limited to women in this instance. Men had only recently begun shaving their faces on a daily basis, thanks largely to the combat requirements of World War I. Gas masks fit clean-shaved faces better, and disposable safety razors became part of the standard issue to soldiers.

FACIAL HAIR

Along with your pubic, underarm, and leg hair, hair can sometimes develop on your face. Or, rather, the peach fuzz that's already there can grow darker, particularly above your lip. Heredity can oftentimes determine hair growth. Regardless, this is not a cause for alarm or shame. Also, it's not uncommon: One in four girls will get some sort of facial hair. The technical term for it is *hirsutism*.

Facial hair on women, like so much other hair on women that doesn't grow directly out of the top of their heads, is sometimes considered problematic. But as with everything else, what you choose to do about it should be what makes YOU feel comfortable.

GOOD-BYE
TO ALL THAT

There are different methods for removing hair on your body, if you decide that's what you want to do. We covered some of these methods earlier, but we'll go over them again where they apply to different parts of the body.

LEGS: Most women who choose to remove their leg hair do so by shaving. If you do this, you should always use a clean razor (NEVER rusty) and soap and water, or shaving cream. Don't ever shave your legs dry, it will irritate the skin and give you something called razor burn—a red, painful rash. You can also wax your legs, which is more painful and can be quite messy if you decide to do it at home, which is why many women opt to go to a salon and spend money to have it done by a professional. Shaving lasts a few days. Waxing can last four to six weeks. Lastly, some women choose to use depilatory creams. As discussed earlier, these creams contain a chemical that dissolves your hair. Basically, you slather it on, wait, and wipe it away. This method also lasts roughly four weeks.

LEGS:

UNDERARMS: The area under the arms is very sensitive, and generally women choose to shave the hair away. Again, use a clean razor and lots of soap or shaving cream. Try and shave in the same direction the hair grows in order to cut down on razor burn. Like with your legs, you can also wax or use a depilatory cream.

FACE: Don't shave. I repeat: Don't. Ever. Shave. If you have facial hair that makes you uncomfortable and you want to get rid of it, the first thing you should do is talk to a trusted grown-up. Your face is a very sensitive area and you don't want to fool around with it. If you decide you want to get rid of it, you can choose between using a depilatory cream made specifically for the face and waxing. Removing facial hair is the most common use of laser removal.

EYEBROWS

Eyebrows have long been subject to fashion whims. The Romans loved a unibrow. They considered it a sign of intelligence. In the Twenties, flappers thought pencil-thin brows were the height of fashion. In the fifties, pinup girls thought bushy brows were sexy.

Eyebrow Fashions THROUGHOUT HISTORY →

ANCIENT EGYPT

ANCIENT GREECE AND ROME

1960s AMERICA

1950s AMERICA

1970s AMERICA

1980s AMERICA

1990s AMERICA

Removing eyebrow hair is more about eyebrow shape. As we noted earlier, it tends to follow fashion fads—thick one year, thin the next. Many, many women never touch their eyebrows. If you do decide you want to remove eyebrow hair, it's a good idea to get a professional to do it the first time. Eyebrow hair does not grow back quickly. You may end up living with these eyebrows (or lack of them) for a long time.

MEDIEVAL EUROPE

VICTORIAN ERA

1920s AMERICA

1940s AMERICA

1930s AMERICA

2000s AMERICA

2010s AMERICA

A FEW MORE SPECIFIC
TECHNIQUES:

TWEEZING: Tweezers have been around since ancient Egypt. They are little tools you can hold in your hand and use to pluck out individual hairs. Many people use them to remove unwanted facial hair, particularly eyebrow hair.

THREADING: A centuries-old technique still in practice that is similar to plucking with a tweezer. A professional uses thread to capture and yank the hair. This method is usually used for eyebrow or other facial hair.

I started waxing my arms and upper lip when I was eleven. I had felt like I looked more like my Indian uncle than other girls. Then, this kid, Daniel, held my arm up in the middle of a school assembly and said, "Look how hairy this girl's arm is." I felt really ashamed of my body. It made me want to be invisible. But, I no longer get embarrassed about my hairy arms. Now I only wax sometimes, and when I do, it's for me, not for other people.

Reshma

I am a very hairy person, and I'm really self-conscious about it. But I found that when I was at camp over the summer, I was totally comfortable. All my friends were girls I knew really well from having spent seven summers together. Being with them, I realized that I just need to accept it— we all have hair.

Eve

I remember when I started getting armpit hair—it felt like a really big issue for me. My friend had borrowed her dad's razor and confided in me that she shaved her arms, legs, and armpits! I planned and planned and planned how I was going to ask my mom for a razor. Then, one day, while sitting on the couch with my parents, I just lifted up my arm and said to my mom, "Hey, look: I have armpit hair. Can you buy me a razor?" I tried to make it really casual, like I had just noticed it. Inside I was freaking out. A few days later I came home and there was a razor on my bed.

Isabel

CHAPTER 5

Shark Week

Look around you. Every woman you see has had her period. And if she hasn't gone through menopause, there's a good chance that she's starting, just finished, or is just about to get her period again. It's funny to look at it that way but there is power in knowing that we're all in this together. What's really magical about this fact is that you don't know *which* of those women around you have their period. That's because even though we all have a leak here and there, no one can just look and see it. It's not plain to the world in any way. It's their secret to hold or share.

Now, this may not seem so helpful when you're in the bathroom and you notice that you have some clumpy, bloody bits coming out of your vagina, but I'm here to tell you it's all totally normal and actually pretty amazing. One day

DOES SWIMMING WITH MY PERIOD REALLY ATTRACT Sharks?

The short answer is **NO.** There is no evidence to suggest that sharks are attracted to people who are menstruating any more than they are attracted to any other human being.

Also not especially attracted to people with their periods? **BEARS.** So swim and camp your heart out every day of the month.

in the future, you may start to look at your period differently. It might grow to be a reminder that your body is functioning as it should. Amazing as it might seem when you're dealing with the mess, embarrassment, and even expense of your period, older women who have gone through menopause say they miss it when it's gone. That's because from the time you first get it, all the way to when you stop getting it, your body operates on a sort of clock, an internal calendar, and every month, unless you're pregnant, the alarm bells go off and—bam—you menstruate. It can be a lot to take in, or get out, as the case may be. And there will be blood. But it's good blood. If blood can be your friend, your period is your bestie. Blood sisters for life.

LET IT
BLEED

*O*kay, now let's get down to specifics. This next section is going to be a bit messy, but I believe every girl should know exactly how her body works. You and your body are in this thing together for the rest of your life. The better you know each other, the happier you will both be.

Here is what is actually happening when you menstruate: Menstruation is part of a monthly process called your menstrual cycle, which is your body preparing itself to become pregnant. Every month, your uterus, also known as your womb, sheds its lining. This lining, which becomes menstrual blood, works its way out of the uterus through a small hole in your cervix, and then out of the body through the vagina. It usually takes about three to seven days for this to happen. This is your period.

But why is your uterus shedding its lining? For this we need to return to your ovaries. In addition to

Women who live together often note that they cycle together, but there is not yet any scientific data to back this up.

THE Female REPRODUCTIVE SYSTEM

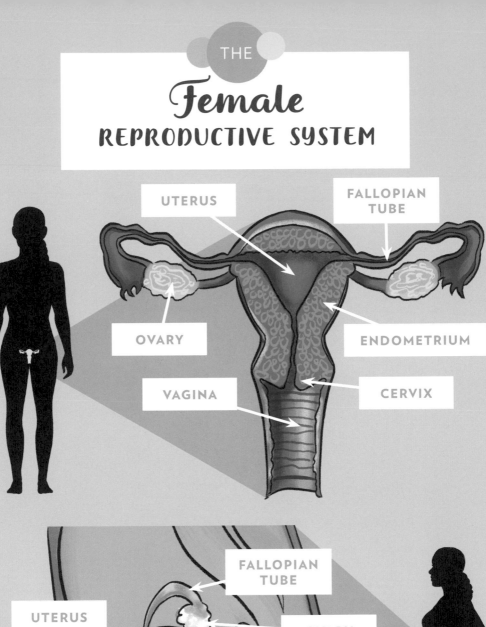

UTERUS

FALLOPIAN TUBE

OVARY

ENDOMETRIUM

VAGINA

CERVIX

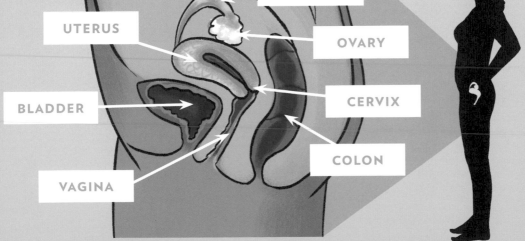

FALLOPIAN TUBE

UTERUS

OVARY

BLADDER

CERVIX

COLON

VAGINA

controlling hormones, ovaries also hold eggs (ova). Every month, midway through your cycle, your ovaries release an egg into your uterus. This is called ovulation. In the days leading up to ovulation your uterus thickens with extra blood and tissue. If the egg is fertilized with sperm, it will attach itself to this extra-comfy wall and begin to grow into a baby. When there is no sperm present, the uterus sheds its lining, along with the egg. This is why, when you are sexually active, skipping your period is sometimes the first sign you are pregnant.

Your menstrual cycle is counted from the first day of bleeding in one month to the first day of bleeding in the following month. This cycle may be a little inconsistent in the first few years you get your period, but as you get older you'll likely begin to recognize all the signs and symptoms of what is happening over the course of the month. The average menstrual cycle is twenty-eight days, but yours may be a few days longer or a few days shorter.

It's not unusual when a girl gets her period for the first time to worry that she accidentally pooped in her pants. Often, the discharge from your first period is more of a brownish color. You're growing up now and chances are you don't regularly poop without knowing it. So remember, if you see something brownish in your underwear, it's probably your period.

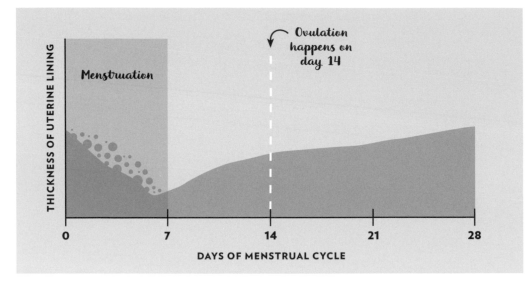

Either during that first period, or your next one, the uterine lining that you are shedding will look different. It won't necessarily look dry and crusty and brown, it will be closer to the color of blood. But it will still look different from the blood you see if you cut your finger or scraped your knee.

I already know what your next question is: When will it come? Or maybe for some of you it's already arrived, and you want to know why it came so soon. I can't answer either question. And neither can anyone else. It will come when it wants to come. But I can give you a *very* general idea: You can expect to get your first period any time between the ages of eight and eighteen, though the average age for *menarche* (the official term for getting your first period) is generally between eleven and fourteen.

Here's another way to look at it: Generally speaking, your period will arrive two years after your breasts begin to form and about a year after you begin to notice pubic hair. You may also begin to notice some discharge in your underpants in the month leading up to your first period.

Super quick diversion because you need to know about discharge. It's the white crusty stuff in your underwear. Everyone gets it; it's not something to be embarrassed about. It's totally normal. I used to find it mortifying even though I knew no one else could see inside my underwear.

Does that help? Not so much? I know it can be frustrating, but if it helps, it's the same for everyone. None of us know. Yes, it can be difficult to be the first or the last person

WHAT'S
Normal?

AGE OF ONSET at 11–14 years old ranging from 8 years old to 16 years old

AVERAGE FREQUENCY is 32 days but 21–45 days is considered normal

LENGTH OF MENSTRUATION is typically 2–7 days

NORMAL BLOOD FLOW requires 3–6 pads or tampons per day

THE AVERAGE AMOUNT OF BLOOD LOSS during a period ranges from two tablespoons to half a cup

in your friend group to get your period. You might want to scream: *Where are you and what is taking so long!* Or maybe: *Why are you here so early, a little warning please!* Unfortunately, your period is not interested in what others are doing, or whether or not it's keeping to your schedule. Your period is more like a houseguest who arrives unannounced, exactly when she pleases and then, without waiting for an invitation, moves into your bedroom permanently, and reads your diary. Just know that it's coming.

And no, there's nothing you can do to make it come earlier.

BUT WILL IT
HURT?

The answer is yes and no. We usually associate blood with some sort of wound, but as I explained above, your period is not a wound. You're supposed to be bleeding. It's healthy!

When you bleed from your period, and aren't wearing a tampon, it mostly feels like you are leaking, which might feel uncomfortable, but it isn't painful. When people complain they are in pain because they have their period, they are almost always referring to menstrual cramps.

CRAMPS!

When women complain about having their period, it's often about the cramps that can accompany it. It's possible there are women out there who haven't experienced cramps before or during their period; I just haven't met any of them yet. The severity of cramps varies from girl to girl, and will often change throughout your lifetime. Cramps tend to be worse in the first few years after you get your period. Some girls get mild cramps, some very extreme ones that can be debilitating.

First let's talk about why you get cramps. As you know, when you get your period it is the result of your uterus shedding its lining. In order to do this the uterus contracts, which is what causes the cramping. Cramps, medically known as *dysmenorrhea*, are caused by prostaglandins, which are released in order to make your uterus contract.

There are a number of ways to deal with cramps, depending on their severity. Sometimes a hot water bottle on your lower abdomen will do the trick. And this may surprise you, but exercise helps. Honest. Walking or swimming when you have bad cramps is often the quickest way to get rid of them. If they are really bad—and I'm not going to lie, they can be really bad—you can ask your parents for a painkiller like ibuprofen. Once you have your period for a few years and get to know it better, you will likely begin to know when you're going to get cramps—the day before; the first day; mid-period—and will be ready to deal with them using one of the above methods.

But what if your cramps are so severe nothing seems to work? This is possible. For some women periods are very painful. If you are one of these women, and you find that your period cramps are continually very painful and de-bilitating, you should tell your doctor. In some instances, very severe cramps can be a sign of an underlying problem. But sometimes they're just cramps. Your doctor will be able to help you figure it out, and also give you ways to deal with it. Just know this is not in your head, and don't be afraid or ashamed to ask for help.

MOON DANCE

Keeping track of when you get your period is a good habit to get into early on. Before we had calendars and clocks, women used to keep track of their periods by the phases of the moon. These days there are plenty of period tracker apps that make this very simple; you just click on the date your period starts and have the option of entering any symptoms you may be experiencing, like cramps, bloating, or heavy flow days. Or you can do it the (semi) old-fashioned way and mark an *x* on a calendar.

Once you do start getting your period, try to pay attention to how your body feels in the hours or days before the bleeding starts. For instance, your breasts might feel tender or you may have some cramps. The more you get to "know" your own body, the more you will be able to predict when your next period will start so that you can better prepare. If you want to wear a pad just in case, that's fine.

Dr. Laura C. Torchen,

ENDOCRINOLOGIST

1. **What are the different hormones that impact menstruation?**

   There is a fluctuation of estrogen levels over the course of a menstrual cycle. The estrogen spikes really high in the middle of the cycle when you're ovulating. After you ovulate, your progesterone levels go up; levels rise during the second half of the cycle, then drop. Estrogen primarily builds up the lining of the uterus and progesterone supports the lining of the uterus to prevent it from shedding. When the progesterone levels drop, that's when the uterine lining sheds and you have your period.

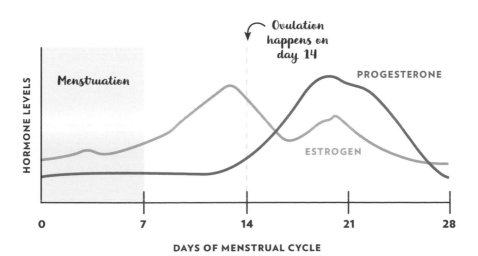

ASK**FLO**

I get discharge before and after my period. I got it before my period even came. Is this normal?

YES! Vaginal discharge is totally normal. And everyone gets it. Discharge is also called cervical mucus. The discharge that comes before your first period, and every month after you have started menstruating regularly, is a result of healthy hormone function and is a sign your body is ovulating normally.

If your discharge has a strong odor, has more of a cottage-cheesy texture, or if you're particularly itchy, you should talk to a doctor; there may be medicine to help.

How do I stop the blood clots in my period?

Most girls are surprised to find that when they get their period the blood doesn't really look very much like, well, blood. We've already spoken about what a period is, the shedding of the uterine lining. You may be a bit shocked to see that your period is sometimes kind of chunky. Yup, chunky. Don't worry, these chunks are soft and they don't feel any different leaving your body than the thinner blood that accompanies them.

These chunks are blood clots, and they occur when the blood sitting in your uterus is waiting to leave through the cervix. You've probably learned about the natural clotting properties of blood in your science class. Well, the blood leaving your vagina clots as well. That's why menstrual fluid is clumpy.

This is kind of a big deal and for some reason it's not often discussed. It's normal for your menstrual blood to look like a clumpy, clotty mess. So don't freak out if you see a chunk.

There are a few things you do need to pay attention to. If the clots are changing over time, if you're bleeding more than usual, or if you have severe cramping, it's always a good idea to visit your doctor.

Will my periods ever get regular?

You'd be amazed how much is considered "in the range of normal" when it comes to puberty. Some girls get their periods at age twelve, and from that point on it comes like clockwork every twenty-eight days. Others get their first period and don't see the Crimson Tide again for a year. Both are perfectly normal.

So what's a girl to do? Plan! You should keep a stash of supplies handy for when your period decides to show up again. Also, don't worry. Over time, most women's bodies regulate and you fall into a consistent period pattern.

But what's a consistent period pattern? Well, it looks something like this:

It arrives every 21–45 days.

It stays between 2–7 days.

You have normal blood flow that requires between 3–6 pads or tampons per day.

You can see that even a consistent period has variations. And what if you don't evolve into something that fits into this range? The most important thing to keep in mind here is that if you feel there's something wrong, talk about it with your grown-up and visit the doctor. Your doctor has seen it all before and can talk to you about the specifics of your situation.

I was twelve, and I was in a restaurant with my family over the summer. I had my bathing suit on, which was a good thing since bathing suits seem more absorbent! I realized that there was something unusual going on, but I don't remember thinking it was a big deal at the time.

When we got home later that night, I told my mom, and she said, "This is a beautiful thing! Let's celebrate!" I remember thinking I was going to die (of embarrassment).

Robin

The first couple times I had my period, it was brown, but I didn't know that that was possible. I got really freaked out and Googled all sorts of things to figure out what was wrong with me. I thought it wasn't my period because it wasn't blood in the traditional red sense.

When I finally talked to my mom, she just gave me pads and said, "Oh, I think you got your period! I'm going to tell your dad that you're a woman!" That was the end of it.

Debra

I started my period three weeks before my sixteenth birthday. It was perfect. So many of my friends had started their periods years earlier or had been counting down the days until they would start, but I was in no rush begin. I was grateful for every month I didn't have to deal with it!

Kiri

CHAPTER 6

MANAGING THE
Mess

"LISTEN UP, LADIES, MENSTRUATION DEMONSTRATION!"

This chapter isn't about all the blood, it's about what you can do to make sure you don't walk around with blood on your clothes. And luckily we live in an age when there are many options. There are disposable pads and tampons, which are the most popular and most widely available products available. There are also reusable products, which some people love for the convenience and the low ecological impact. We'll cover them all.

The average woman will use over 16,000 tampons in her life.

A LITTLE HOMEWORK
ASSIGNMENT

It's possible you've done this before with a friend or family member, but I'd like you to take a stroll down the feminine care aisle in a drugstore or supermarket. You'll notice a few things.

First, people tend not to linger in this aisle. *But that doesn't make sense*, you might be thinking. There are so many products, how can you decide what's right for you in less than three seconds? There are a few reasons. Mostly, people just aren't comfortable being spotted (Get it? Spotted!) in that aisle. Why people are self-conscious about it is a mystery I've been trying to solve for the better part of the last five years. We all know that every girl gets her period, so it really shouldn't be anything to be embarrassed about. If this book does its job, you will be able to linger casually in the aisle and make informed choices.

The second thing you might notice is there are a LOT of different products. Pads, liners, tampons, cups, the list goes on and on. And each product comes in a myriad of sizes and shapes. It can be confusing to a newcomer. It takes a few cycles to figure out what works best for you, so don't get discouraged.

The last thing you might think when you see the aisle is *"Wow, being a girl is expensive!"* You are right about that. Some studies put the total of how much the average woman will spend on her period over her lifetime at more than $18,000 dollars. That's a lot of money.

Now, if you're frugal or you worry about the ecological impact of all these products in the supermarket, there are options for you. These options require getting a bit more up-close-and-personal with your blood. That may be just fine with you, or you might think it's gross. As with everything else in this book, however you feel is the right way for you.

AND NOW A LITTLE
HISTORY

The disposable sanitary napkin was first created in the late 1800s by French nurses on the battlefield who discovered wood pulp bandages stopped excessive bleeding. In 1896, the manufacturer Johnson & Johnson picked up on this and created their own version called Lister's Towel: Sanitary Towels for Ladies.

Up until 1969, the year man landed on the moon, women used a belt to hold their menstrual napkin in place. Fortunately, 1969 was the year of important discoveries and pads with adhesive tape were first introduced. One very large step for women's comfort level.

Cultures as far back as the Egyptians have recorded women inserting materials, such as soft papyrus, into their vagina to absorb menstrual blood. The modern tampon, however, was created by Dr. Earle Haas in 1931, and patented as Tampax. After failing to

Cleopatra and her friends may have used tampons.

get anyone interested, he sold the trademark and the patent to a woman named Gertrude Tendrich, a German immigrant who lived in Denver, Colorado. Tendrich promptly hired women to manufacture the item and nurses to lecture on its benefits, then began selling it in drugstores in Colorado and Wyoming. Today the Tampax brand is still one of the biggest tampon brands in the world. That's the history of tampons, or as we like to say, HERstory.

The first time the word "period" was said on television, referring to menstruation, was in a Tampax ad in 1985. The person who said it, Courteney Cox, later went on to star in the hit TV show *Friends*.

Period Management
THROUGHOUT HISTORY

ANCIENT EGYPT — Women may have used papyrus tampons.

ANCIENT ROME — Women used wool tampons.

ANCIENT JAPAN — Women used paper tampons held in place with a bandage and changed them 10–12 times per day.

1896 — Johnson & Johnson began selling the first sanitary napkin: Lister's Towel.

1931 — Dr. Earle Haas patented the modern tampon and called it Tampax.

1933 — Gertrude Tendrich bought the patent for Tampax and hired women to produce them.

1969 — The adhesive pad was invented, and women could finally stop wearing menstrual belts.

TOOLS OF THE
TRADE

- **MENSTRUAL PAD:** This is a thin pad made out of layers of absorbent material that has adhesive tape on the back so that it sticks to your underwear. When you're changing your pad, that sticky tape helps you roll the pad up and wrap it in some toilet paper. There are also reusable menstrual pads which you need to wash in the washing machine between each use.

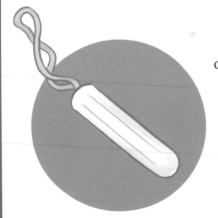

- **TAMPON:** A tampon is a tube of absorbent material inserted into the vagina either with an applicator or using your finger. Tampons are a safe and effective way to manage your period blood, but keep in mind that it's very important to change your tampon regularly—every four-to-six hours, depending on how heavy your flow is.

Many people think tampons are flushable and that's why they like to use them. In fact, that's wrong. Unlike toilet paper, which is designed to disintegrate when submerged in water, tampons stay intact. So please, just wrap them in toilet paper and dispose of them in the trash. Plumbers will thank you.

- **MENSTRUAL CUP**: The menstrual cup is a small, bell-shaped cup made out of silicone that you insert inside your vagina to catch the menstrual blood. When you remove it, every 4–12 hours depending on how heavy your flow is, you dump the blood in the toilet or sink, wash the cup under running water, and then replace. One cup can last for a number of years, and needs to be sterilized in boiling water at the end of every cycle. This is a product that you'll probably discuss with a grown-up first.

- **SEA SPONGE**: Yes, that kind of sea sponge. This is used by gently wetting the sponge so that it's flexible and then inserting it into the vagina. After a few hours it's removed, rinsed out, and reinserted.

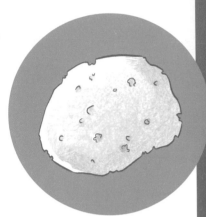

- **PERIOD UNDERWEAR**: This is a recent addition to the period tool kit. This is special underwear that is constructed of material that can absorb your period so you don't have to use a tampon or pad. On your heavier days, you can use this underwear as a backup with a tampon or pad so you don't have to worry about leaking through.

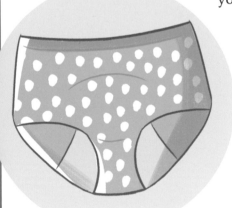

YOU ARE
LUCKIER
THAN YOU KNOW

This next bit might blow your mind. In fact, it's inspired hundreds if not thousands of people to take action. In many countries girls miss school when they have their periods. And it's not because their cramps are too bad. In some countries where poverty is rampant and access to sanitary protection is slim, girls who are menstruating don't go to school. Often the schools don't have proper bathrooms or the girls' families simply cannot afford to buy the adequate supplies she needs to make it through a day while she's bleeding.

In countries where access to needed supplies is limited, girls and women sometimes use paper or old pieces of fabric to catch the blood when they are menstruating. They may not even have access to sturdy enough underwear to hold the rags in place. And while some women in the United States have now decided that "free bleeding" is empowering, for these girls, it's incredibly limiting.

Think about how quickly you'd fall behind if you missed one week of school every month. The consequences are pretty devastating, and that's why there are so many people now committed to helping these girls stay in school.

One organization solving this problem that I've come to know and love is Zana-Africa. In addition to manufacturing pads for sale, they distribute period packs to girls in East Africa. These period packs have underwear, enough pads for a semester of school, and a comic book that teaches the girls about their periods. Distributing these packs helps these girls stay in school and graduate.

Photo courtesy of ZanaAfrica

Use a Tampon

No one, and I mean no one, is born knowing how to use a tampon. I can almost guarantee that if you ask ten women how they learned how to use a tampon at least nine of them tell you a story that involved their friend, sister, or cousin outside the bathroom door coaching them through the first insertion. Some of them might even tell you that their friend actually put the first tampon in for them. It's that tricky. But just like riding a bike—once you know how to do it, it seems so simple. So let's get started.

First of all, for newbies, a tampon with an applicator is usually recommended. The applicator is smooth and is easier to put in. Remember if you're using a tampon with an applicator, the applicator is just that, it's not meant to stay in your vagina. The tampon is actually a pretty small cotton thing with a string that is inside of the applicator.

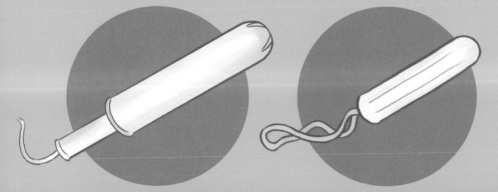

**TAMPON
WITH APPLICATOR**

**TAMPON
WITHOUT APPLICATOR**

STEP 1: Wash your hands. Tampons and tampon applicators are sterile when you take them out of the package. Keep them that way by handling with clean hands.

STEP 2: Next, get out a mirror and take a look at your vulva (outer vagina) and your vaginal opening. Don't be afraid, it's a part of you. Find your vaginal opening; it's designed to be stretchy. Try inserting the tampon (in the applicator). If that's scary, use your finger first so you can see how totally non-scary it is.

    If the mirror thing really freaks you out, you can skip it. Just use your finger to feel around for the opening.

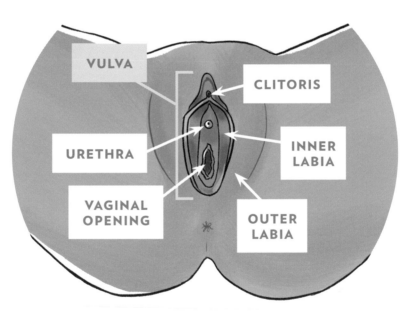

VULVA

CLITORIS

URETHRA

INNER LABIA

VAGINAL OPENING

OUTER LABIA

STEP 3: Once you've gotten up close and friendly with your vagina, put one leg up on the toilet seat, place your thumb and middle fingers on the ridged part of the applicator and gently glide it in until your vulva (the technical term for the "lips" surrounding your vaginal opening) is touching your fingers.

STEP 4: When you get there, all you need to do is use your index finger to press the skinny little tube that's still sticking out of you.

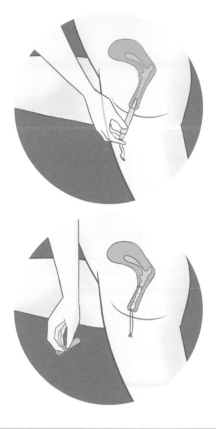

STEP 5: Voilà, you are officially wearing a tampon! Remove and dispose of the applicator. The string should be visible outside your body, and this is the part you'll use to remove the tampon later.

You might want to practice it outside your vagina first so you can see how the mechanics all work, then go for it! We strongly recommend sacrificing one of those cotton ponies to the period gods so you can see what they look like. It's much easier to insert a tampon if you know how it works.

Once you become a regular, you will be able to do this very quickly while sitting down on the toilet.

Last thing to note here:
Tampons aren't for everyone and that's totally okay.
Pads are always an option.

A NOTE ABOUT

TSS:

TOXIC SHOCK SYNDROME

SINCE WE'RE TALKING ABOUT TAMPONS, IT'S IMPORTANT TO TALK ABOUT TSS.

The good news is that TSS is very rare. It's a complication of having a staph bacterial infection in your vagina. Symptoms of TSS can occur quickly and without warning. They include a fever, low blood pressure, vomiting, diarrhea, muscle aches, and headaches. There are hallmark skin changes, which include a characteristic rash mainly on your palms and soles resembling a sunburn. Swelling and ulcerations in mucous membranes such as your eyes, mouth, and throat are also possible skin changes of TSS symptoms. If you notice any of these symptoms it is an emergency. You should immediately remove your tampon and then see your health care provider.

ASK**FLO**

Can I lose my virginity if I use a tampon?

I get asked this question all the time. And the answer is quite simple: no. The only way to lose your virginity is to have sex. Using a tampon can sometimes stretch or even tear your hymen, which is the thin membrane that can cover part of your vaginal opening. But it's important to remember that some girls are born without a hymen, and many, many girls don't have a hymen by the time they reach puberty; it's been worn away by sports, or horseback riding, or even just walking or cleaning yourself, or all of the above! Any girl that gets her period can use a tampon if that's what she wants to do.

Can I start wearing a pad even if I haven't gotten my period?

Pads are designed to absorb blood when you are on your period. But many girls are worried that their period will come and catch them unprepared. If this is you, and wearing a pad will make you feel more comfortable or confident, then go ahead. As with many other things we have already discussed, what makes you feel good is the right thing.

If you feel like a pad may be too much you can also use a panty liner. Panty liners are basically mini pads designed to keep your underwear clean of discharge.

I didn't use a tampon until college. My mother and sister didn't use them so I never really thought about it. I was at a job during the summer when I got my period unexpectedly. I was with my best friend, but she only had tampons. So she stood outside the stall and talked me through how to use it. That was when I learned that my vagina was a different hole than my urethra (where pee comes out).

I started using a DivaCup in college, at the recommendation of my very eco-conscious sister. There was an initial learning curve to getting the cup properly placed and suctioned tightly, but I've now been using it for over five years. Between the enormous cost savings, the environmental benefits, the convenience of fewer trips to the bathroom, and the freedom from stocking and carrying supplies, I'm never going back!

CHAPTER 7

MIND THE

Gap

We've spent a lot of time talking about your body, but in my opinion the biggest changes that take place during puberty is with your mind. Let me explain.

Until recently, you were a small child. As a mother, I can tell you that small children look at the world as it affects them. They are very self-absorbed. That's not a bad thing; it's how their brains work. As you age, you start to become more aware of how the world responds to YOU instead of just how you respond to the world.

Let me give you an example. When you were five you may have left the house wearing a crazy combination of costumes and

> **When** you're awake, your brain produces enough electricity to power a lightbulb.

colors and you wouldn't even care that people took notice. You weren't dressing that way for anyone other than YOU. My guess is that now you are more likely to think about how your friends, family, or even strangers would think about what you chose to wear. Your sense of style hasn't necessarily changed, but your *awareness* of what other people are thinking has increased.

MEET YOUR
BRAIN

W e're going to talk about your brain and how it develops. This is critical information that I didn't have until I was already a grown-up. Once I learned about this stuff, I realized how helpful it would have been to know all of this when I was still a kid. That's why I'm sharing it with you.

Brain food:
Human brains have the same consistency as tofu.

What you're about to read is an introduction, a vastly simplified overview of brain function and development to help you understand what's happening. This is not a complete explanation; it's really just broad strokes.

Think of your brain as your command center. In this command center there are approximately 100 billion neurons. Neurons are cells that transmit information through your brain.

Your brain, and its neurons, perform important functions and are responsible for your behavior, feelings, and judgment.

Your brain completed approximately 95 percent of

its development before you were six years old. Your brain, like your body, had a major growth spurt. Right now, while you're going through puberty, your brain is having another growth spurt, and the pathways that make connections between your actions and your brain are further developing.

Have you ever seen a plasma globe? It's a clear glass ball with a mixture of gases and an electrical current. When you aren't touching the outside of the globe, it looks like a bunch of small lightning bolts coming from the center. Then when you touch the outside of the globe, the bolts come together to form fewer, stronger bolts. Your brain

develops much like a plasma globe. There are bolts, or neu-ral pathways, in every direction. Then, like someone's hand is placed on the globe, the smaller neural pathways disap-pear in favor of fewer, stronger neural pathways.

During puberty, it's as if there are a few hands being placed on your plasma globe to make fewer, stronger bolts. Here's an example. If you really love to play a musical in-strument and you keep playing throughout your adoles-cence, those pathways will become permanent and you'll likely keep playing that instrument, or at the very least maintain the skill, for the rest of your life. But if you stop

MILESTONES IN
Brain Development

AGE 0

BRAIN SIZE: 360g

A newborn baby's brain is about a third of the size of an adult's brain, but it has the largest number of neurons it will ever have: 100 billion!

AGE 1

BRAIN SIZE: 940g

A baby's brain more than doubles in size by its first birthday.

AGE 6

BRAIN SIZE: 1200g

A six-year-old's brain is about 95% the size of an adult's, but it's not fully developed yet.

AGES 10–15

BRAIN SIZE: 1270g

Your brain reaches its adult size during puberty, but don't be fooled: It's still developing.

AGE 30

BRAIN SIZE: 1290g

Congratulations! You have an adult brain.

playing and practicing during adolescence, those pathways will slowly get weaker or even disappear. The cells and connections that are used frequently will survive and flourish until they essentially become hardwired. But the paths that aren't used are the small bolts that disappeared. These pathways don't have to be lost forever; you can always learn new skills or relearn those that have been lost. But your chances of hardwiring skills increase if you work on them throughout your adolescent brain growth spurt.

HOW THE
COMMAND CENTER
MAKES DECISIONS

*T*he way your brain is developing also impacts the way you make decisions.

There are two parts of your brain that are critical to decision making: the **PREFRONTAL CORTEX** and the **LIMBIC SYSTEM.** Think of these two parts of the brain like this: The limbic system makes decisions based on emotion, and the prefrontal cortex makes decisions based on logic. The tricky part for you is this: Your prefrontal cortex, or rational brain, is not fully developed until you are about thirty years old; those bolts in the prefrontal cortex are just starting to get stronger. But your limbic system bolts are nice and strong.

THE LIMBIC SYSTEM

The limbic system is the part of the brain that controls your emotions. It controls your tears and your laughter and your anger. This part of the brain will be pretty much fully developed by the time you go through puberty.

Your limbic system wants you to feel good. It's the part

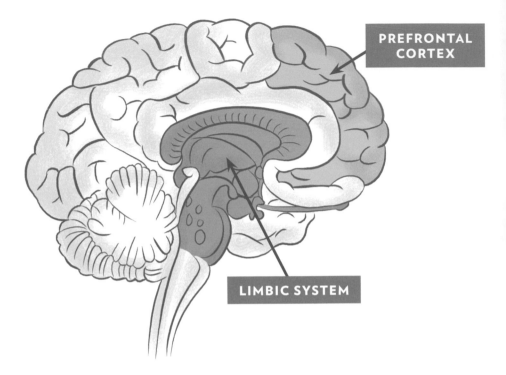

that loves your friends. Because it's fully developed before your prefrontal cortex, your rational brain, sometimes it can get you in difficult situations. For example, when you're with your friends and someone has an idea to do something fun, but perhaps risky, your limbic system will get excited to ride along. Since it's fully developed, it might get to a decision quicker than your prefrontal cortex. Your fully developed limbic system plays a big role in the peer pressure adults worry about.

Another great example of how to understand this distinction is to think about using helmets. When you're a little kid you wear a helmet when you're riding a scooter, riding your bike, or skiing, rarely challenging your parents. But when you get a little older, sometimes helmets seem less cool. Your brain hasn't gotten stronger or more resistant to concussions if you fall. But you are making decisions for yourself and you are choosing what *feels* good, not necessarily what's the safest. That's your limbic system talking without getting feedback from your prefrontal cortex.

It's nothing to be ashamed of. When I was a teen it wasn't considered cool to zip up a winter coat and wear a hat. I still recall freezing outside with my friends in the winter because I was more concerned about pleasing them than I was about staying healthy. My limbic system won a lot back in those days.

THE PREFRONTAL CORTEX

As we discussed, the prefrontal cortex won't be fully developed until you are roughly thirty years old. Yes, thirty! For many of us, that's after we choose to begin families. Hard to imagine, right?

The prefrontal cortex is in charge of making rational decisions. When you were little you needed your grown-up to tell you not to touch the stove because it was too hot and you'd get burned. The prefrontal cortex is the part of your brain that tells you these sorts of things as you get older, so you don't need your grown-up around all the time to make sure you don't get hurt.

Brain development, **AGE 6**

Brain Development Spectrum

LESS DEVELOPED ——————→ **MORE DEVELOPED**

In this diagram, the red and yellow areas of the brain are less fully developed, while the blue areas have reached their adult state. Even though the older girl (on the right) has more blue and green areas in her brain than the younger girl, her brain won't be completely finished growing until she's about thirty.

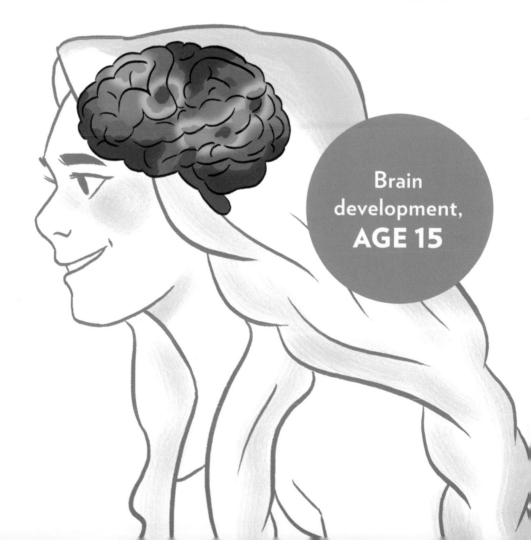

Brain development, **AGE 15**

This is important so I'm saying it again:

> **The part of your brain that is responsible for making rational decisions is not fully formed until you're thirty years old.**

As you get older, the decisions you're faced with are more nuanced than whether or not you should touch a hot stove. Also, the really complicated decisions are often made with your friends who we know now impact your limbic system. That's why this is such critical information.

An undeveloped prefrontal cortex is not a get-out-of-jail-free card. You're still on the hook for all your actions. You remain responsible for you. However, it does mean you might have to work harder in order to make good decisions.

When you're a grown-up all these parts work together at the same speed. When you're going through puberty, it can sometimes feel a bit like your limbic system is in charge.

SO WHAT'S A GIRL
TO DO?

For one thing, be patient. When I said your prefrontal cortex won't be fully developed until you're thirty that doesn't mean that it's not capable of making good decisions. What that means is that it operates more slowly than the other parts of your brain. So while the emotional part of the brain is moving quickly, the prefrontal cortex is sluggish to respond.

There is one thing you can do to help you make better decisions: slow down. Give your rational brain a chance to process and catch up. Find a quiet place and really think about your decisions. You'll be glad you did.

HORMONES
AND MOOD SWINGS

So now that you understand how your brain development affects your decision making, let's complicate matters by talking about hormones. You already learned earlier in this book that hormones control things like breast development and pubic hair. Basically, your hormones are the sun in the universe of puberty.

To begin, here's a quick reminder of the basics: Girls have ovaries. Ovaries make the hormones estrogen and progesterone. Alternately boys have testicles and testicles make the hormone testosterone. There are many other hormones in the body, but when we talk about puberty these are the ones that matter.

The tricky thing about hormones is that they can also affect your brain and your mood. Shockingly, there have only been a few studies that directly link hormones to mood, but it is generally considered fact among doctors that hormones can give you mood swings and might make you irritable.

Here is how *I* know that the impact of hormones is real. Every month, before my period, I get PMS. For me, the PMS takes two forms: headaches and emotions. The day before my period, like clockwork, I always get a very bad headache. It's usually how I know I should sleep with a pad on because for sure I'll wake up bleeding.

But what happens a few days before the headache is that I start to feel more sensitive. TV shows make me cry. I worry about what people around me think. And my brain goes on overdrive when I'm trying to sleep. This is my personal experience, yours will likely be different.

Hormones can impact more than your mood. For some women the hormonal fluctuations before their period cause food cravings. Chocolate, anyone?

Once you start getting your period regularly, you may notice that you feel a certain way at a certain time of your cycle. That's because the hormones follow a routine each cycle. Estrogen spikes when you're ovulating and progesterone spikes before your period. These hormone spikes may impact your mood.

EVEN GREAT WOMEN
HAVE PMS

Remember that emotional PMS I just told you about? Well, that surge of emotions has been one excuse other people have used to keep women from positions of power. You may have heard someone say that a woman can't be president because she can't be trusted to make important decisions when she's PMS'ing. I want to dispel that myth once and for all.

Even though I get "the feels" right before my period arrives, it doesn't mean that I am not responsible for my actions or am somehow unable to operate. In fact, at least part of this book has been written while I was menstruating. And

I go to work and run HelloFlo even on days when I'm bleeding. You know who else gets their period and still slays? Tay-
lor Swift, Beyoncé, Emma Watson, Malala, and every female
Olympian in history to name a few. I'm guessing that Beyoncé wouldn't cancel a concert because she's bleeding. She
still gets herself onstage and appears #Flawless. And there's
no way Malala lets her period stop her from changing the
world, one schoolgirl at a time.

Dr. Laura C. Torchen,

ENDOCRINOLOGIST

1. How do hormones impact mood?
People usually accept that changes in mood are part of the pubertal transition, but in terms of what really causes some of those mood changes, it's not well worked out.

The biggest emotional change that parents report are mood swings and irritability. They report that everything makes their child feel emotional. For example, kids get angry or sad very easily. They lash out at their parents for things they would typically not have lashed out at them before.

Ever since I started going through puberty, controlling my moods has been a bit harder for me. Sometimes I get upset or angry and I'm not even sure what caused it. I know I'm more sensitive than I used to be. My family calls me the mean-ager. I know they're only joking, but when they say it, I get really angry at them. It doesn't help that they usually say it when I'm PMS-y or feeling really moody, so it's hard for me to be anything other than mad.

Julie

One of my friends in ninth grade started hanging out with another group of friends who were into experimenting with drugs and alcohol. She was doing all of these things that I just couldn't bring myself to do. I realized that it wasn't a good situation for me. When she wanted me to join her, I said no. It helped that I saw it coming, so I had already prepared myself in advance and knew how I wanted to handle it.

Isabel

CHAPTER 8

ALL THE
Feels

If you were to look at a book about puberty that was written when I was growing up, you probably wouldn't find a lot about emotions. That's because complex emotions were not really something many people talked openly about until fairly recently, especially when it came to younger people. But I think it's so important to talk about your emotions—how they feel, how to manage them, and when and how to ask for help.

Do you ever wake up in the middle of the night feeling worried, except you're not sure what about? Do you have a test tomorrow? A race? A class speech you've been thinking about and practicing? Maybe your stomach aches or you find your mind darting from thought to thought and you can't stop.

Or maybe you're worried about bigger stuff. Things that feel out of control and won't go away. Maybe you worry you are not good enough, or smart enough, or pretty enough. Maybe if your hair was shinier, longer, straighter; your teeth were bigger, smaller, whiter; your hips were narrower, rounder; your legs longer, shorter, shapelier; maybe if your test scores were higher, you ran faster, sang better. Maybe then these feelings would go away.

You know what I'm going to say right? You are great just how you are. You may think your grown-ups just say this because they're obligated to, but it's actually true and you should listen to them.

A certain amount of worry and mood swings are normal. We've already talked about your hormones, and how sometimes it feels like you are on a roller coaster. And there are so many things bombarding us throughout the day that it can sometimes be hard for your brain to stop. Sometimes you just want to cry. You are a human being and there's lots of stuff going on in your body, and in the world around you, that is brand new. Honestly, it would be a little weird if you weren't anxious about it.

Okay, here's where I let you in on another huge secret. One thing I've learned as I get older—and actually this may be the other number one most important thing I've learned in my life, so listen carefully—all the things you're worried

about are probably being worried about by many, many other people right this second. I'm serious. You think you're too weird and no one has ever felt like you? I'm sorry to tell you (sorry, because I know that sometimes it feels good to think you're the only one ever) but someone out there has felt exactly what you're feeling right now, and has been worried about the exact same thing. In fact, probably more than one person. In fact, probably someone right this second. Everyone feels like you do at some point in their life. Even famous people. I'm not sure who decided we should keep it such a secret. But now you know! Feel free to pass it on.

It's normal to be anxious about things. It's normal to feel alone, like you're the only one. This happens to be extra

true when you're going through puberty. Right now you are being bombarded with more things than at any other time in your life—in your brain AND your body. I've been giving you a lot of information so far in this book, so maybe let's just stop for a second and remember: Puberty is hard! Not just because of what your body is doing, and not just because of what your brain is doing, but also because while all these things are happening to you, the world is pounding you with information and questions and expectations and tests and warnings. If there were a cartoon about puberty, it would be a picture of you riding a unicycle, while juggling and singing opera, and then being handed a math test on top of it, and all the while there is a huge clock counting down behind you. Hurry up! Be better! Go faster! OR ELSE.

Here are some things that I have found are helpful for me when I'm feeling anxious.

TIPS TO HELP
CALM YOUR MIND

DO SOMETHING YOU ARE GOOD AT OR ENJOY.
Everyone is good at something. This includes you. It doesn't matter what it is—it could be writing poetry or skateboarding— just set aside some time to do it.

TALK TO SOMEONE. It doesn't have to be a parent. It could be a friend, or a guidance counselor (that's what they're there for, after all), an aunt or uncle, an older cousin, a coach. Look at the adults in your life and pick the one you feel most comfortable with and just sit and tell them what's on your mind. Chances are they have gone through something similar.

THINK ABOUT WHAT YOU WOULD TELL A FRIEND if they told you they were feeling bad. Sometimes we are nicer to other people than we are to ourselves. Stop for a minute and imagine one of your friends came to you and told you they were feeling bad about all the same things that you are feeling bad about. What would you say to them? Chances are you would be very kind and understanding. Now try it on yourself.

SPEAKING OF FRIENDS. Remember how we said you are probably not alone in feeling like this? There's a pretty good chance that your friends are going through the same things you are and may need someone to talk to about it, also.

PUT DOWN YOUR DEVICE. When I'm worried or nervous I often turn to my phone to occupy my mind. But even if I start with a meditation app open, I usually end up looking at my social media feed and getting worked up about what is going on in the world. Before I know it, I've wasted an hour looking at other people's lives. Sometimes this distraction is a perfect antidote, but other times it can leave me feeling like my life isn't as great as it should be. That's not helpful. For me, sometimes the best thing to do is put the technology down and go for a walk. For you, maybe it's coloring or beading or any activity that helps you focus your mind.

BUT SOMETIMES IT'S
MORE

There are a lot of points in this book where I've told you that if you feel something is really wrong it's important to talk to your grown-up or a doctor. The same holds true for your feelings. If you feel like you're really struggling emotionally, it's important that you talk to a trusted grown-up and get some help.

If you're wondering how to know if you need help or if what you're experiencing is "normal," the answer is not super simple. But hopefully this will give you some guidance. According to psychologist Dr. Lori Evans, the symptoms doctors look for when determining if a person needs outside help include a sense of hopelessness and losing interest in things that you used to like. Dr. Evans says, "If it's affecting how you are functioning—we know something else is going on."

Psychologists I interviewed while writing this book emphasized that the goal is not to avoid difficult emotions; the goal is to learn you can actually manage difficult emotions. Speaking with a grown-up or a professional can often give you the tools you need to learn how to cope with sadness or anxiety.

Dr. Lori Evans,

PSYCHOLOGIST

1. **If I'm sad does that mean I have depression?**

   Sadness is a normal part of life, and for all adolescents the sadness can be intense. That said, if the sadness is causing impairment, meaning a teen cannot do work in school or they are having significant social problems or they are hopeless regarding the future, or possibly they are losing interest in things they previously enjoyed doing, it may be more serious. The confusing part for parents is that being depressed does not mean someone will "act" depressed 100 percent of the time. Their teen maybe can't rally the energy to go to school, but then they go out with their friends on Friday night and seem happy. That can still be depression. Because of the variable nature of adolescent moods, we are sometimes thrown off course. When diagnosing depression, we look for a sense of hopelessness, possible suicidal ideation, the idea that you have lost interest in things that you used to like, and any significant changes in sleeping and eating habits.

2. **Is there any one thing that you find yourself repeating over and over to parents or kids?** Asking for help is a good thing! As much as possible, destigmatize the idea of getting help or asking for help. You know, my best success besides when I help reduce symptoms is when my patients tell me that they are open with their friends about their therapy. They aren't hiding it.

3. **What should I do when I'm feeling bad about myself?** Ask yourself "What advice would you give a friend who was struggling with this same problem?" Start early with self-care. Self-esteem comes from being competent in something and feeling good about it. Find the things you are competent at. When I say competent, you don't need to be the best person on the travel soccer team. What do you feel good about doing? You can always fall back on that when everything else has gone kaput. Sometimes I ask patients to write it down or I ask them early on to make what we call a self-care kit. This could be a playlist of songs that makes you happy, a food or smell you love, anything that makes you happy and helps you to change your mood.

Colleen Drobot,
FAMILY THERAPIST

4. **Why do I suddenly feel so much?**

   It's around this age that most kids start to develop reflective consciousness. That's the ability to think back on your thoughts or actions and feel something about them. For example, you may feel happy or sad, or maybe disappointed in something you did. When you come into puberty you feel like you're living in a fishbowl—and it's all because of that reflective consciousness. As a younger child you didn't really have this awareness, but now it's developing.

5. **How do I know if what I'm experiencing is normal angst or if I need help?**

   If you're having a hard time, the most important thing is that you don't feel alone. You should have at least one person who is a grown-up that you can go to for help. If you feel like no one gets you, or that you have no adult in your life that you can talk to, that is when you want to get help. You need someone in your life who you like and trust. Research shows that you only need one caring adult to help you get through these periods.

There was a time when I was thinking a lot about therapy. I felt like I just had this weight on my chest that I was constantly carrying around. Then, one Saturday morning, I told my mom that I thought I needed to see a therapist. My mom called one of her friends to get a referral.

I remember after the first meeting I felt so much better, like a little of the weight had been lifted. I think what therapy has taught me is that you can't argue with your feelings but once you express them and put them in words it gives you another perspective on the situation.

Because I developed so much earlier than my peers, my parents brought me to a therapist. I remember hearing that my mother was concerned because I'd spend a lot of time in the bathroom putting on makeup to hide changes in the way I looked. Thinking about it now, though, I realize that I was super anxious about changing and other things, which was why I spent hours trying to cover up what I looked like.

I had a really rough time in middle school—there was friend stuff, family stuff, and personal stuff. I didn't like the way that I felt in my body. As it was changing I always found something that wasn't good enough or that I thought was a flaw. During puberty you look in the mirror and sometimes just think everything is wrong.

CHAPTER 9

THE SISTERHOOD OF THE
Traveling Periods

When we talk about great love stories—tales of passion, hate, loyalty, companionship, true love; all the things we deem most important and worth fighting for in life—we are almost always talking about romantic love. But for most of us, our friendships with other women are just as important. These are the real deal relationships. The ones that get you through the best and the worst of times. These are the friendships that help you figure out who you are, and then become who you want to be. These are your friends who share such deep, deep roots that no matter how hard you yank on them they can't be uprooted.

They are and will be the most amazing relationships in your life.

Which is not to say they are easy. They are hard. Sometimes they are cruel. Yes, cruel. Maybe you know this already. Maybe you are reading this and thinking, *girls are the worst*. And you're right. Girls can absolutely be the worst. I don't think there's a single girl in the wworld who, at some point in her life, hasn't for no apparent reason had all her friends turn on her and shut her out. If this has happened to you, you know it's *the worst*. It is horrible. It is so horrible you will probably remember it for the rest of your life, even when you are old and gray, and when you think of it you will shudder.

And when you are old and gray, you will tell the story to your best girlfriends and they will tell you about the girls in their school who were *the worst*. And while you may not laugh about it—some things will never be funny—you will be grateful for the women friends you lean on now, and wish you could time travel back and tell your younger self it doesn't just get better. It gets to be the best. The absolute best.

It may seem strange that I'm choosing to end this book about puberty with a chapter on friendship, but that's exactly what I'm doing. You see, I was young once and I remember how my friends both lifted me up and sent me spiraling into great sorrow. Now that I'm older and know a lot more about how our brains develop and what it feels like to have hormones coursing through your body, I understand that the worst years for friendship are often those that are smack dab in the middle of puberty. Coincidence? I think not!

So girls, I'm going to leave you with some stories from girls and women just like you. They all survived middle school. And every last one of them came out on the other side stronger and even more committed to the power of female friendships. Because even though we have the capacity to be awful, sometimes in the end, we learn that we are all stronger when we're together.

As you travel through the winding road of puberty, just remember to always be kind to yourself and to your friends. You'll be here a while, so try to enjoy the awkward.

xoxo,
Naama

When I was in the fifth grade there was a period where all the girls "got dropped," i.e. iced out for a couple weeks. It was brutally painful. I still remember it. I also remember doing it to another girl before it happened to me. Awful. I wanted to fit in so badly so I was mean, until it happened to me. But I only needed to learn that lesson once.

Naama

Having girlfriends will save your life. Seriously.
You should have friendship ambitions the same way you're
ambitious about your career and personal life. The women
in my life that are so supportive and honest about the world
and society that we live in don't just care about our lives, but
also other women that face oppressions that we don't face—
and they do something about it. Those are the women that
you need in your life. Find them, cherish them, fight for
them, and show up for them.

Chaédria

I remember a terrible year in which I raced to get to school early because, for some reason, whoever was the last to arrive became an object of torment throughout the day.

During that year, I found sanctuary in a life outside school that was interesting and exciting (with completely different people). Singing lessons—with the camaraderie of endless rehearsals with supportive, funny, creative people— made the drama at school seem boring and taught me the magic of dancing to my own tune.

Marci

I had a big fight with my group of school friends at the end of the school year in eighth grade. I went to camp thinking that I would come back and have no friends. Then my camp friends and I talked about it a lot, and they made me realize that I had to stop blaming myself for the whole problem. They taught me that if you are in a situation and everyone is making it look like you are the problem, it's probably not only *your* problem. You need to realize that you are good and that it's not your fault. There are always other people involved.

My camp friends will be my friends for the rest of my life. They are so special that I don't need to see them every day, but I know they'll always be there.

I still vividly remember the girl who I had befriended when she first moved to town not six months later telling me, in front of EVERYONE (well, a busload of kids), that she couldn't be friends with me because I wasn't popular enough. There was also another girl who tormented me all through high school, but with whom I am now Facebook friends, in part, because I now understand her own high school journey and the family situation that she was dealing with that none of us knew about back then.

Kathleen

Something positive happened to me after I fell out with my friends when I was ten. It hurt like hell. But when it happened, I remember making the decision to never rely on just one group of friends again. So I've ended up meeting people from all walks of life and having diverse, beautiful, and great friends from different backgrounds, countries, and interests who have taught me so much. It pushed me to get over my shyness. And if it hadn't happened I don't think I would have evolved the way I have and have all these different, eclectic, and incredible people in my world.

Chrysi

There was one time that I was really being bullied about the hair on my body by a group of boys, and the popular girls came over to me to ask what was wrong. Those girls—who weren't even my friends—started to defend me. They yelled at the boys and started pulling up their own sleeves to show the boys that everyone had hair. They stood in solidarity with me, and I'll never forget it.

Kate and I have been best friends since ninth grade. There's no one else who gets my shorthand or my references to our high school geometry teacher or who remembers that unfortunate perm I had at age fourteen. And because she knows me so well, Kate is the only person I trust to give me advice, to tell me honestly what she thinks without making me feel judged or hurting my [feelings].

Acknowledgments

So many people were involved in the making of this book. First and foremost, Glynnis MacNicol who worked tirelessly on the manuscript with me and who taught me about finding vulnerability and truth in writing.

Emma Parry, who saw a book where I didn't and pushed me to write it. Julie Strauss-Gabel, who believed in this project, gave it shape, and pushed me hard to find and use my voice. Melissa Faulner, who I was lucky enough to catch in her cube on a few occasions and took the time to answer my novice questions. Anna Booth, whose creative direction was inspired, and Fleur Sciortino, whose illustrations brought this book to a whole new level. The whole Penguin Young Readers crew who understood why this book had to happen.

Olivia Merns Berger, who spent a year filling up Costco carts with me as we were making HelloFlo a reality. Jill Bressler, who designed the HelloFlo logo because she believed in me and what I was doing. Natalie Cosgrove, who kept me sane and kept HelloFlo going during many highs and lows. Lily Herman, who we'll all be working for one day and who gathered testimonials during her last semester in college.

Dr. Cara Natterson, who advised me as I was building HelloFlo and taught me so much about parenting, puberty, and brain development, and to whom I will forever be grateful. Dr. Sheryl Ross who is a true vagina warrior.

Many of the people we interviewed or who volunteered their time to read the manuscript for medical accuracy: Dr. Lori Evans, Dr. Laura Torchen, Dr. Stephanie Nichols, Dr. Robert Malenka, Dr. Eve Koltuv, Colleen Drobot, Kiran Gandhi, Sarah Murnen, Megan Grassell, and Patricia Cartes.

The incredible PBS Frontline series, Inside the Teenage Brain, which should be mandatory viewing for every teen and every parent of a teen, and which filled in so many blanks for me as I was learning about brain development.

The ladies of The List, who are always in my corner. Especially Rachel Sklar, who understood that we needed an "old boys club" for women and created one.

Emily Habert, Melanie Kletter, and Sarah Schriever, who stumbled through puberty with me and were the inspirations for Camp Gyno.

Thank you to David, who is the most tireless supporter and partner I could ask for and who has learned more about periods in these past five years than most women learn in a lifetime. And to Orly and Micah for being my everything. And finally, thanks to the most important women in my life: my mom, Judith, and my sister, Liat, who were my real-life puberty guides and taught me that there's nothing my body does that should cause me shame.

ABOUT THE AUTHORS

Naama Bloom is the founder of HelloFlo.com, a modern-day health site for girls and women. Her mission for HelloFlo was to create a place where women and girls could learn about their bodies in an open and honest environment without any shame and with a healthy dose of humor. HelloFlo's first two videos, "The Camp Gyno" and "First Moon Party," have been viewed over 50 million times and show girls that while puberty can be awkward at times, it can also be fun and empowering. She lives in Brooklyn, NY, with her husband and two children. *HelloFlo: The Guide, Period.* is her first book.

Glynnis MacNicol is a writer and cofounder of TheLi.st. She is the author of the forthcoming memoir *No One Tells You This.* Her work has appeared in print and online for publications, including ELLE.com, *The New York Times, The Guardian, Forbes, The Cut,* and *Town & Country,* among others.